RECLAIMING THE GODS

Reclaiming the Gods

Magic, Sex, Death and Football

By

Nicholas R. Mann

GREEN
MAGIC

Some of this material first appeared in 'The Dark God' by Nicholas R. Mann, Llewellyn, 1996

This first edition published in 2002 by
Green Magic
BCM Inspire
London WC1N 3XX

Typeset by Academic and Technical, Bristol
Printed by Antony Rowe

Cover Design by Chris Render
Cover Artwork Nick Williams
Technical Assistance R. Gotto and Richard Fraser

ISBN 0 9536631 8 3

GREEN MAGIC

Contents

1

Introduction

The Goddess is. She reaches out and is all things. The earth, the underworld, the heavens, the universe, are all within her sphere. The God moves through her. He moves through all she is. He undertakes the journey through Life, through birth and death. He knows the way through her earth and sky. He uses craft, science, learning, mathematics, law, art and technology to find the way. He is the guide. He is the lightning flash. He is the God revealed in Life.

For many years in the Western world we have had a God, a singular, all-powerful deity, but who is the God? He, and his myths and images, like those of the Goddess, hold a respected place in other cultures and in our past, so why is he, like the Goddess, mostly abhorred, feared or neglected in our world today? There is either a silence around the God, or a fragmented and distorted image of him emerges in the horror stories and films that feature the figures of our nightmares. The God appears as Count Dracula, Frankenstein, the Werewolf, Darth Vadar, Sauron – the personifications of our ideas about everything that is unlike and other than God.

While adoration of the Goddess was never entirely relinquished in Western culture – Mary and the Black Virgin being cases in point – the God has sunk so low in our estimation that he has become the objectification of evil itself. The ancient Gods have become Devils, stalking the world, seeking to corrupt the souls of us mortals. Rather than being, as they were in the past, Gods of nature, of animals, of wealth, of fertility, of craft and inspiration,

7

of divine aspects of ourselves, the Gods have become the definitive figures of evil, terror and fear.

The God is, in fact, taboo. He is one of the most difficult subjects to talk about. He is a subject full of contradictions. If someone says they are performing actions in the name of a God other than the one in the Bible or are accused of committing a deed in one of his names, the media sensationalise it, priests denounce it, fundamentalists see it as further evidence of the Satanic plot to take over the world, and police organise special units to investigate it (finding nothing). While at the same time, actions are performed in the name of God involving wars, terrorism, torture, persecution, disenfranchisement, discrimination, expulsion, indoctrination, ecocide and genocide that are eagerly accepted and participated in by millions.

The 'Light,' I was told as a child, is the quintessence of spirituality. A Creator, an eternal almighty God, an ethereal figure 'up there,' surrounded by haloes, meteorological glories, and other composed and shining presences, was the picture provided for me of goodness and of God. The world, the forest, the cave, the night, the unmentionable places 'down there,' strong emotions, and the horned and clawed creatures of the natural world were, by contrast, portrayed as the domain of wickedness and evil. They were of the Devil. This was extremely confusing. From my childhood perspective, I could not feel the negative effects of any demon – in fact most 'demonic' things felt rather pleasant – while I was extremely aware of the cruelty, intolerance, and punishments inflicted upon me in the name of an eternal God of transcendent light.

Although it is quite right and proper that evil actions are decried and good ones applauded, why has our thinking about them been forced into this strange framework? What is the reason for the oppositions of good and evil, light and dark, spirit and nature, to be thought of in terms of an objectified God and the Devil? And, furthermore, by what history did we arrive at the identification of these values with characteristics that are masculine?

A great moral evaluation is placed upon the fundamental, but in themselves quite neutral polarities of sky and earth, spirit and matter, male and female, light and darkness. They have come to symbolically represent other entirely unrelated things. This is, I believe, a great shame, and does us a great disservice even as a metaphor or an allegory in a story. But I don't think someone is ever going to lean over to me and say: "Why, you don't actually believe in all that stuff about god in heaven or the devil in hell, do you? We just made it up to get the kids to behave." No.

The lost and distorted figure of the God in fact opens up a world of great depth, transformation, vision, and compassion. The full mythic image of the God and all his aspects provides a connection with wholeness, with life, and thus with all things. His presence as symbol enables movement around the whole cycle of existence. His shining ambition, beauty and incisiveness allow him to reach the heights. His fertile presence in the fields, woods and oceans brings abundance. His cool, shadowy, underworld allows release, integration and fulfilment. It is not a Creator God outside of life found only in a book or in sermons that we need, it is the God one with life who inspires and excites us and gives meaning to our experience.

In particular, the restoration of the God with all his aspects means the reintegration of the masculine with life. The return of the whole God allows the possibility of envisioning the whole man. The God restored suggests a new life-affirming male spirituality and the renewal of the relationship to women, perhaps envisioned as the Goddess. The God restored provides an exemplary pattern for some of the greatest challenges that men now face: the balance between masculine and feminine, the letting go of the desire to consume and control to the point of self-destruction, and the healing of the separation between life and spirit.

Before the advent of transcendental monotheism posited one god 'up there' and, by implication, his counterpart 'down there,' and identified the former with good and the latter with evil, a much bigger world existed for us all to live in. Light and dark, above and below, spirit and nature, were not seen as being good or evil, but as necessary parts of a whole. The old polytheistic and mythic worldview had no need to personify good or evil in particular deities. It had no need to separate the creator from the creation, to take spirit out of life. Each God and Goddess was present in and was revealed through the complexity of life; and, like life and the humans who made them, each divinity had many complex, subtle, and sometimes paradoxical aspects.

The monotheistic worldview worked as though the linguistic part of our minds which functions in a simple yes or no, up or down, friend or foe mode, was given hegemony over the whole world. Our conscious, literal mind – not our deep, subtle, analogical subconscious – then went berserk. It proceeded to schizophrenically categorise everything into black and white compartments. A categorisation which dark-skinned people, women, forests, chasms, wolves and snakes, in fact all animals – and the inner archetypes such as the 'shadow' – have felt to their cost ever since. The lopsided doctrinaire dualism of a good god and a denied shadow is a great shame, for it amounts to disinheritance.

The loss of the whole God means an enormous loss not only to the wholeness of the masculine but also to the wholeness of all life on earth. Because of the reification of a single aspect of the divine masculine and its subsequent literalism by religion, we are disinherited from the full polymorphic, earth-rooted wisdom of our ancient ancestral traditions. Because of the denial of the dark, shadowy archetypes that are a vital part of the constellation of our total being, and especially because of the projection of them outside of ourselves, we – perhaps a majority of the human race – are in a state of mental, emotional and spiritual disorder. We persecute ourselves. We discriminate against others, and denigrate and exploit most life forms. We are 'sinners.' Others are 'heretics.' The creatures are 'lesser' than us. They are 'lower' on a hierarchical scale. With this worldview we ruthlessly exploit animals and the environment for our material gain. The objectified God-and-the-unmentionable-other worldview engenders acts that fall far short of the full mode of life that we are meant to live.

If there is any identification of evil to be found in these pages, it is not in an active or an external devilish principle. If anything, it is the repression of our ancient mythic spiritual tradition, and a general failure on our parts to fulfil all that we are capable of being on this rich, life-abundant, planet earth. If there is any identification of good, it is not found in literalising an old dogma or repeating a tired belief. It is the rediscovery of the ability of subtle and complex mythic images to motivate our commitment to act in life from their provision of value, meaning and goodness.

The book proceeds in sections that describe an aspect of the God. Each section, like this one, concludes with a description of the God taken from various places around the world. I focus on European, Near and Middle Eastern Gods who are likely to be familiar to the English-speaking reader. I describe some other deities, but in general have not gone into the huge realm of African, Australian, Chinese, Native American or Polynesian deities as these are outside of my experience. The book does not have to be read sequentially. By using the index all the references to a particular God can be found. Should the reader chose to read the book through however, the descriptions will assist in building up a comprehensive picture of the God restored.

Shiva – Shiva or Siva, is the God of the Dance, of Death and Fertility. His many aspects reach back far into the pre-Brahmaic past, making him one of the most ancient of gods. In the ancient aspect known as Rudra he is the Wild God, the Horned God, the Lord of Beasts. He is blue faced, and clad in the skins of animals. His posture in representations from the 3rd millennium B.C.E. Indus civilisation is cross-legged, like that of the Celtic God Cernunnos.

In his terrible form he is the destroyer of the universe. In his beneficent form he is shown in sexual embrace with the Mother Goddess. She also has many forms; among them are Kali, Parvati, Durga and Devi. He is represented by the Lingam, a cylindrical rounded stone. She is represented by the Yoni, a flat or concave circular stone with a rim. The Lingam is the still centre of the Wheel of Existence which the dynamic energy of the feminine turns. As the creative power of Nature, the symbols of their union include the Sacred Tree.

In ecstatic sexual union with the Death Goddess Kali, supreme annihilation is brought about. Kali is shown with a decapitated head, or is decapitating Shiva's head. From this point, only total transformation and regeneration is possible. In one Vedic tradition, Shiva is castrated and his phallus/lingam eternally fixed to the earth. Shiva is the giver of wisdom, the divine teacher, a musician, a

11

wanderer, a cobra, and the Father of Demons. He carries a trident and is accompanied by a bull.

In the Aryan cosmology imposed upon India after 1500 B.C.E., Shiva becomes the Destroyer in the Hindu Trinity. He is also a somewhat dark and devious God of Love.

Pan – The Arcadian Goat God. The Roman Faunus. Half-man, half-goat, the origin of Pan is obscure. Some say Hermes as a ram fathered Pan on a nymph, or, less poetically, that Hermes seduced a goat. Others have Pan as a child of the ancient Cronos and Rhea, or they adopted him, making him a foster-brother of Zeus.

Pan, like the Wild Herdsman, guards flocks and herds, beehives and the forest. Pan may mean 'shepherd' or the shepherd's crook. He is called upon to encourage animals to reproduce. He is the ancient God of Fertility. He assists hunters, but his favourite pastime is sporting with nymphs and Dionysos's drunken Maenads. His chase of the elusive Syrinx caused the creation of the Panpipes when she hid from him as a reed. His true love is Selene, the Moon Goddess.

Pan is father to Silenus, the old teacher of Dionysos and the Satyrs. Pan possesses the art of prophecy, coaxed from him by Apollo, who is the only one to better Pan in music. Pan is roguish, jumpy and excitable. He can cause panic, and his shout makes crowds go out of control. Like the Gruagach he hates clothes and insists on participants coming naked to his rites. He is ambivalent, causing love and seduction, disorder and harmony.

Kokopelli – The phallic, seed-carrying God of the American Southwest and northern Mexico. Kokopelli carries the seeds of life in his hunchback. A Trickster, seducer, and eternal wanderer whose annual visit ensures seasonal fertility. The sound of his flute always heralds the arrival of Kokopelli. He leads the dance to the fields to break open the ceramic containers of seeds upon the ground. The breaking open of his hunchback means his death brings wealth.

2

Guide to the Underworld

The God is the hunter. He enters into the spirit of every living thing. He knows the pathways of the soul, and is there anticipating its moves. He strikes and a part of him dies. He shares a mystical communion through his extraordinary sensibilities with every living thing. He strikes, never missing, at every human soul, and escorts them to the door of the Underworld. He is Charon, Herne the Hunter, Gwynn ap Nudd, the Rider of the Wild Hunt.

One of the first and most notable aspects of the ancient mythic image of the God is that he is a guide to death and the underworld. The God is a doorkeeper, a Guardian of the Threshold, a ferryman, and a psychopomp, the 'conductor of souls.' He guides the soul to the entranceway and then around the realms of the dead.

In the history of humankind, the earliest images of the divine are the Great Mother Goddess. She appears in every aspect of life. She, in her many prehistorical representations, is identified with birth and death, often to the exclusion of all other physical characteristics. Her fertile breasts, vulva and buttocks are emphasised, or she is the stiff white figure of death. Although it is hard to know how the role of the God was differentiated during these early times, as compared to the Goddess there are so few representations, he does eventually emerge as her son and her lover. It is he who undertakes the journey around her Great Round. It is he who loves, dies and is born in the arms of the Goddess. He goes into the Heavens, the Earth, and the Underworld on a cyclical basis.

In later myth, in folklore, and in early history, the God emerges as the guardian and protector concerned for the well being of the individual soul undertaking the journey of birth, life and death. He is especially concerned for the soul travelling in the Underworld domain of the Goddess. Examples of this god include Gwynn ap Nudd, Hermes, Thoth, Masau, Sukunyum, Anubis, Jizo and Yama. A black horse, a bull, a wolf, or a dog is often his companion. It is his responsibility to guide the soul through the dark and nebulous regions of life and the after-life.

As he emerges in history, and as consciousness emerges from out of the totality and primal unity of the Goddess (see Table 1), the God gains more distinctive individual characteristics. He can be addressed as Lord of this or that particular domain. He becomes Lord of the Forest, or Lord of the animals, or a sky or a solar god. Gradually his earthly, dark, chthonian functions become distinct from the otherworldly, bright and heavenly. The god who is the guide to the underworld, of winter and the night, comes to mirror the god of the heavens, of summer and the stars. The two evolve together with the growing perception of the distinction between humanity and the Earth Goddess, concurrent with the process, expressed linguistically, by which the world is cosmologically ordered in terms of pairs of opposites.

With the ascendancy of the patriarchal Light God in the time of the first Western civilisations, it is a hero who undertakes the journey to the Underworld. The hero defeats the Dark Winter God and his accompanying monsters, ensuring the victory of the Light Summer God. The God of Light thus defeats, once and for all, his protagonist in the Underworld. This is the situation we find ourselves in today – an ascendant, in fact, a transcendent God, and a denied, suppressed and feared shadow. The redeeming saviour god emerges in history as a function of dualistic consciousness. As the divine is now outside the creation but is responsible for it, the representative of the divine has no alternative but to appear in life as its heroic redeemer.

In this condition, the God is no longer a guide to the soul through all the dimensions of the Great Round. God is now a vicarious, external entity, mediated and defined by others. The man is fragmented and no longer possesses the vital key for the journey into the shadow within his being. Wrong action is seen as the fault of another and redemption is possible only through the action of yet another being, a saviour. The enemy, the other, salvation, authority, validity and wholeness are all outside the self. The prevailing notions around theism, belief in the Gods, are embedded in a worldview that is so inherently dualistic and dogmatic that we have reached the point of divorce from meaningful reality. Contemporary theism frequently asks for belief to be based on faith alone, even at the expense of the observation of reality, as for example in Creationism. It is possibly only through the examination of worldviews outside our own, either in our past or in other cultures, that we can step outside of prevailing theistic notions of the sacred and find those that still provide meaning.

The Celtic Druidic tradition for example provides an alternative perspective. It is not a religion as it has no gods or goddesses – at least not in the sense we understand them. It has no creation mythology, no creator, no dogma, no dualism of earth and spirit, and thus no fall, no sin, no redeemer and no need for redemption. The sources reveal that the Celtic Druid tradition is based upon being: being in life – being a part of the stream of the vibrant, perfect and pure experience of life – and coming into the many forms of life, again and again. In this view, the gods and goddesses are immanent aspects of life. They are divine presences that pervade particular domains. They are accessed through symbol, through story telling, through immediate experience. The old woman figure for example is the symbolic aspect of the Goddess as the universe, the mother is the presence of life throughout the universe, and the domain of life on earth finds expression in the aspect of the Goddess as the young woman. The latter has many symbolic aspects. She may represent sovereignty, the spirit of place, the ancestors, the tribe, the animals, and so on. The male figures in the Celtic cosmos emerge as presences in nature, as aspects of life, and most often as figures on an eternal quest – perhaps a game or a hunt – seeking the fullness of experience that life offers. The deities of the Celtic tradition are presences within life, while life itself was a quest to satisfy the longing of the soul in the discovery of itself and the object of its love in the ever-changing forms of existence. The Grail Quest was perhaps the last flowering of the rich mythos of Celtic consciousness, and, as in other equivalent

Table 1. Time scale of Eurasian Deities and Mythic Consciousness

Time period	Deity	Mythic Consciousness
1. Early Paleolithic 0 to 25,000 B.C.E.	Great Round	Primal, undifferentiated Great Round.
2. Paleolithic 25,000 to 9,000 B.C.E.	Great Mother	Differentiation – but all things, including male and female, contained within Great Mother.
3. Early Neolithic 9,000 to 5,000 B.C.E.	Great Goddess	All things: birth, life, death, male and female, within the sacred body of the Goddess.
4. Neolithic 5,000 to 2,000 B.C.E.	Goddess and Son-Lover	Goddess of All, within whom a Son is born, lives and dies. She has several different forms.
5. Bronze Age 2,000 to 800 B.C.E.	Goddesses and Gods	Many Goddesses, beside whom the Gods journey into the above and the below.
6. Iron Age 800 to 0 B.C.E.	Goddess, Earth and Sky Gods	Gods fertilise Goddess, and compete with each other as Lords of Earth and Sky.
7. History 0 to 2,000 B.C.E.	Sky/Light God	Earth God banished by Sky/Creator God. No relationship to Goddess except to birth son.
8. Current Era	Sky/Light God	God rules by word alone. The Goddess and God sublimated. Goddess returning?

This table is not meant to be read as a factual guide. It is meant to give a rough sense of a geographically and chronologically varying sequence. For example, the Bronze and Iron Age shifts in deity and mythic consciousness took place at different times in different places.

The table can be summarised as follows:

(1) At first, human consciousness does not manifest any distinct image of the divine. All is contained within the undifferentiated uroboric consciousness of the "Great Round."

(2) The perception of the divine emerges in myths and symbols of the "Great Mother."

(3) As differentiation increases the Great Mother begins to be seen as the "Great Goddess."

(4) As that which undergoes the transformative processes of her all-inclusive body, the God emerges as the son and lover of the Great Goddess. He is her generative spirit personified as a god of vegetation and animals.

(5) Distinct aspects of the Goddess and the God emerge with the development of language and eventually the growth of literary forms.

(6) The mythic images of the Goddess and the God become subject to the dualism inherent in cultures emphasizing the rational-logical mind and are divided. At first the two extremes of the God – the Light or Sky God and the Dark or Earth God – compete. They remain within the field of the Goddess and typically divide the year between them.

(7) For reasons yet to be fully explained (the political power of ruling male elites?), the Sky God achieves dominance. He is reified to an absolute position. As Creator he is beyond the world. The creative role of the Goddess(es) is appropriated. The Dark Earth God becomes the repository of all that is denied. He is identified with the "other," with evil and the enemy. He becomes the Devil. A bipolarity in mythic consciousness occurs that cannot be reconciled in the fragmented image of the Great Goddess.

(8) It follows that for consciousness to internalise its projected extremes – light and dark, good and evil and so on – it must (a) reconcile its polarised imagery of the God, and (b) recover the whole image of the Great Goddess.

16

mythic traditions, its figures emerge as archetypes constellating the full garden of human experience.

Gwynn ap Nudd – British God of the Underworld, Leader of the Wild Hunt and the Dark Lord of Winter. Gwynn is King of the Tylwyth Teg, the Welsh Fairies. He is the son and lover of Arianrhod, 'Silver Wheel.' Gwynn ap Nudd's name literally means 'White Son of Dark.' White is the colour of bones and death. Nudd or Nodens is a British King of the Underworld.

In Gwynn, writes the *Mabinogion*, is "set the energy of the demons of Annwn." Every Beltane, Gwynn fights with his perpetual rival, the Sky God Gwythyr ap Greidyawl. They compete for the hand of the Solar Goddess Creiddylad. As a Serpent God of the Waning Year, Gwynn returns to the earth at Beltane in a boat-shaped oak coffin. He re-emerges six months later at Samhain. His origins probably lie in his role as a Neolithic mortuary deity – the Lord of the Necropolis.

As a leader of the Wild Hunt, Gwynn guides the riders and their hounds (originally wolves?), the red and white Cwm Annwn, to seek out the souls of the deceased. He escorts the dead to the Gates of the Underworld. These lie upon the Isle of Avalon, or on any isle in the Western Sea. Gwynn is specifically located on Glastonbury Tor, a cosmic axis between the worlds. The Tor is also the location of one of the Celtic Cauldrons of Regeneration – later the Holy Grail.

Charon – Etruscan God of Death and the Underworld, adopted by the Greeks and Romans. Charon is the Ferryman across the River Styx to the Underworld, for whom a coin is traditionally put in the mouth of a corpse.

Osiris – In his earliest forms, Osiris is a Tree God, a River God (the Nile) and a God of Fertility. He was known as the 'Bearer of Grain' and the creator of civilization. Eventually he became Lord of the Cycle of Life and Death, moving between "the Heights and Depths." As the Ram-headed God of Death and the Underworld, Osiris is the judge and the bestower of abundance for resurrection. He rules over Tuat, the Land of the Dead. With his brother Set,

Osiris forms all the pairs of opposites: drought and fertility, dark and light, life and death, etc. He is the brother and husband of the Goddess Isis.

Tricked into a casket by Set and thrown into the sea, the corpse of Osiris drifts to Byblos. There an Erica tree encases it. The tree is incorporated as a pillar in the palace of the local king. Found and returned to Egypt by Isis, the corpse is discovered by Set. Assuming the form of a boar, Set cuts the corpse into fourteen pieces (the days of a lunar waxing or waning phase). Every year Isis seeks to find and restore the body of Osiris. She never finds the penis, but succeeds in replicating it in order to conceive Horus. Osiris thus rises as his son Horus, the Hawk-headed God, and daily and yearly meets Set in combat and conquers him.

According to ancient Egyptian texts however, in the "Sphere of the Eternal" where there is no duality, Osiris and Set, light and dark, life and death, are one. This is the secret of the "two combatants . . ." "Whether I live or die I am Osiris." Osiris is the seed as it is swallowed by the earth, the corn as it is cut down, the grain as it is ground and fermented, the moon as it waxes and wanes.

Osiris is associated with the planet Venus and with the Cult of Apis or Serapis, the sacred bull. A column, sometimes with eyes or lopped branches, often represents him. He is the oldest child of Geb and Nut.

3

Judge

The God is the guide to the shadow side of the self. He is the revealer of truth. Before him all are exposed as profound and shallow, loving and envious, high and low, brave and cowardly. He is the guide through the dark emotions, the primeval, reptilian forest, the dank roots of criminal neglect and decay. He is the seer, the protector, the judge, and the measurer of the fullness of the soul.

Closely associated with the ancient mythic God in his aspect as guide and guardian to the dead is the role of the God as Judge, or the Weigher of Souls. Anubis, Osiris, Hades, Math, and Yama, for example, appear in this manner. The Celtic God Math is said to be absolutely impartial, with "no trace of vengeance." He has a wand, that when laid on the ground, means those who step over it can only tell the truth. In the Egyptian tradition, Anubis the jackal headed God, guides the dead to the Great Hall of Judgement. The dead walk over a floor of black and white squares that represent the need for balance in the life of each soul. The God then weighs the heart against a feather.

According to the ancient Egyptian text *The Book of Pylons*, Osiris is the ruler of Tuat, the Land of the Dead. Through the centre of Tuat runs a river beside which dwell hostile beasts and demons. The Boat of the Sun sails through the twelve regions of Tuat, which correspond to the twelve hours of day and night. The boat is guided by Wepwawet, the wolf headed god, the "opener of roads." Through the aid of these deities, the deceased passes through the ordeals of the twelve regions and comes to be worthy of life with Osiris.

In the Western world, the role of the God as judge of the dead is one that appears to have developed fairly recently in historical time. Anubis, as the desert-dwelling jackal, guided the dead in pre-dynastic Egypt, and only with the expansion of the cult of Osiris did he become a judge. The role of the God as a judge in general is older, although this is open to debate. The role of Apollo for example as a God of Light and Truth, may have not developed until the advance of the codes of law in pre-Classical Greece (7th–5th centuries B.C.E.). Lugh, a Celtic equivalent of Apollo, also appears to have entered the pantheon of deities later, although this could be a development of his earlier functions. Apollo and Lugh may have begun life as deities of sun and fertility, before becoming upholders of the codes of law. The older and mainly female deities they replaced were concerned with battle, revenge, 'blood for blood,' and feuding. It is interesting to note however, that once the systems of law were established in both cultures, they were presided over by female figures. Athene presided over the law courts of Athens, and to this day the figure of Justice, as a blindfolded woman balancing scales, stands over the law courts of the old Celtic countries and those of their diaspora.

The point of the system of law instituted under Lugh, which became encoded in the Brehon Laws of Ireland, was that it was restorative and not punitive. Rather than seeking to encumber society with further loss or burden by punishing the wrongdoers, it made it incumbent upon them to set the matter right. Every transgression had a prescribed price, which the transgressor was required to pay. A stolen sheep for example was paid back in kind plus interest, or if several sheep were stolen, then their equivalent might be paid in cattle. Even a slaying in war, say by a member of the warrior elite, meant he had to pay the amount prescribed by the codes to the victim's relatives. The God provides the exemplary pattern for justice, checking the vigilantes wish for revenge, and making sure those responsible for crime are not made more dangerous but encouraged to integrate into the collectively upheld order of society.

Although some might read the ascension of Apollo at Delphi as a landmark in the progression of an oppressive patriarchy, the rise of the symbolic aspect of the God as judge has helped in the establishment of systems of justice throughout the world. Although failing miserably on many counts, especially through its perversion by the rich and powerful, the establishment of codes of law has contributed hugely to society, and weakened the tendency to justice through an 'eye for an eye.' The application of the intellect in the development of techniques for restorative justice, non-violent conflict resolution, mediation on every level, protection of human and animal rights, compliance with international law, and the spread of fair and equal elections, promises enormous and perhaps the only hope for the future. This aspect of the God, exemplified by the stories of Lugh, Math and Apollo in mythology, is one to be proud of and worthy of continued envisioning and development.

In the Eastern world, the role of the God as judge frequently went in another direction. The nature of sprituality there did not tend to the excessive externalization as in the West, and Gods such as Mara and Yama are seen as internal aspects of the self bound up with laws of karma. It is not so much perceived that it is the God as judge who is determining the fate of the soul, as it is the soul itself. There is no external judge, tempter, compulsion, or predestination to do good or evil. The disposition to good and evil comes from each individual, who know their true status when all else is stripped away. This view is probably also at the heart of the esoteric Egyptian teaching of Anubis, and of the Goddess Maat.

These rich mythic traditions of the God in his role as a judge are a long way from the punitive character of the God in the Bible. They are empowering, allowing access to values and validation from within each individual rather than from dogma without.

Anubis – The Egyptian Jackal-headed God who participates in the judgement of each soul. Anubis guides the soul to judgement and weighs its heart against a feather. In funeral ceremonies, the priest as Anubis advocates the revival of the dead. In the Cult of Isis, Anubis is the Psychopomp, the conductor of souls. Anubis is the son of Osiris and Nephythys, sister of Isis. It is said Osiris mistook Nephythys, lover of Set, for his lover Isis, and so conceived Anubis. Anubis is the Protector of Sea Farers, Guardian of Tombs, God of the Summer Solstice and the "opener of roads to the north." The

Greeks identified Anubis with Cerberus, the three-headed hound of hell. He is the dog companion of Thoth.

Math – A benevolent Welsh King of Gwynedd and Celtic God of the Underworld. His name, Math ap Mathonwy, means 'treasure' and 'bear son of bear-like.' Math presides in the domains of justice, wisdom, wealth, enchantment and magic. He will teach any who request his aid without discrimination. Despite the errors of his nephew Gwydion for example, Math teaches him, and Gwydion develops into a great magician. Math is all seeing and nothing can be said that he does not hear. His particular art is the shamanistic one of shape shifting. He transforms himself and others into the forms of animals in order to bring justice. It is his magic that caused Llew Llaw Gyffes to undergo his death and metamorphosis upon the oak tree. He possesses a magic staff that reveals the truth.

Apollo – Greek God of the sun, the arts, and healing. Twin brother of the Goddess Artemis. Among his deeds, Apollo slew the Python of Mount Parnassus, took control of the prophetic sanctuary of Delphi, and brought the muses there. He was said to have beaten Pan in a musical contest. Apollo was enormously popular in the Roman world and his cult spread widely, especially into Gaul and Britain. At many Celtic shrines he was associated with the local deity of the sun and healing.

Lugh – Lugh, 'shining' or 'bright one,' Lámhfada, 'of the long arm,' is a solar deity and as Samildanach he is the 'master of every craft.' As the son of Cian of the Tuatha De Danann and Ethlinn of the Fomor, and fostered by a queen of the Fir Bolg, Lugh blends all the races of Ireland. He is a foster-father to Cuchulainn and foster-son of Manannán. His festival of Lughnasadh, originally a month in duration, now celebrated on August 1, was the time and place for games, for trading, for exchanging contracts, for ratification of Beltane or 'springtime' marriages, and for judgements to be made.

Lugh appears at Tara to help the Tuatha De Danann in the hour of their greatest need. He organises their army, inspires them to fight, and brings with him magical objects such as the boat of Manannán and a sword which will cut through anything. Under the wisdom of his rule, and the establishment of law, the country thrives and the people prosper. His arm reaches everywhere, and the light of his truth illuminates the land. Lugh eventually steps down from the kingship and goes to dwell in the Otherworld. From there he occasionally helps his protégés. He stood in for Cuchulainn against the armies of Ireland for example, while the hero slept for three days.

Lugh is the 'Golden Boy.' Like Apollo, he does not age, nor do satire, abuse and accusation stick to him. The ruler that replaced Lugh, the Daghda, the 'good god' or 'good father,' and Zeus, the father of Apollo, have, by contrast, all kinds of tarnish added to their reputations. Lugh, Apollo, and their local representations (for example, Mabon, Apollo Belenus, Apollo Grannus etc.,) remain bright, shining, youthful, and healing. It was these aspects of the God that were enormously popular in the Roman Empire, and led to the spread of the cults of Mithras and Christ. Christ easily assimilated the earlier and other functions of the God, and, as a judge, a dying and rising god, protector, craftsman and so on, he rapidly entered the hearts of believers as the pure, good, youthful son of the unassailable God.

4

God of Wisdom

The God is Lord of the Night, the full and the dark of the Moon. As the enabler of gestation, change and transformation, he is the source of enchantment, inspiration and creativity. Energy flows up through him, from the darkness of the earth within, to emerge as dance, poetry, music and song, as well as comedy, tragedy, bawdy and lewdness. Raw energy is transformed within his being, to flow up through sex, heart and emotion, to emerge from the head as words and the mind as knowledge.

The aspect of the God that appears as a judge originates in his much earlier role as a God of Wisdom. The ancient Hebrew demon-god Asmodeus was originally the builder of the Temple of Solomon – the exemplary wise ruler. This is the God who knows how to weigh things up, how to carve stone into the six sided ashlar – the fundamental building block of creation. The Ibis-headed God Thoth possessed the magic formula that enabled the dead to find their way around the Underworld. Thoth, one of the most ancient of the gods, is the Egyptian God of Wisdom. He presides over the realms of magic, of music, and of medicine, as well as writing, astronomy and geometry. He is the Divine Judge, and the measurer of all things.

The wisdom of the God begins with the knowledge of geometry, which means 'the measure of the earth.' Geometry itself is said to begin with trigonometry, which means 'the measure of triangles.' This was fundamental to the builders of the pyramids, the Egyptians, from whom the craft of Freemasonry is said to derive. The Greek mathematician, Pythagoras, the first to use the words geometry and trigonometry, is reputed to have spent twenty-two years in Egypt being initiated into its science. The famous theorem, attributed to Pythagoras, that the sum of the square of the hypotenuse of every right-angled triangle is equal to the sum of the squares of the other two sides, is the most important and most used of all geometrical theorems. In a Masonic allegory, the sun and moon, as the two sides of a triangle beside the right angle, represent the male and the female. They shed their light upon their product, the 'Blazing Star' of the hypotenuse. In the Egyptian tradition, the hypotenuse is the divine child, Horus.

The counterpart of Thoth in the Greek tradition is Hermes. Both Thoth and Hermes are conductors of souls around the Underworld realm. Hermes was, from extremely ancient times, represented as a phallic God in the form of a stone rooted in the earth. He is rooted in the earth – rooted in its measures and science. Math has a similar role in the Celtic pantheon. Math is the benevolent God who dispenses wisdom and justice. His absolute impartiality helps every suffering being. He distributes wealth, teaches magic, and his wand of truth is also the 'king's measure' – the yardstick from which all other measures derive. In the Nordic traditions, Odin, who was also identified with Hermes, is the giver of wisdom, of language, and of memory. He gained his wisdom from his journeys into the Underworld.

From his deep source of knowledge rooted in the earth, the God gives the wisdom necessary for each soul to find their way around every part of creation.

Asmodeus – Like Lucifer, Asmodeus is a fallen angel, a seraphim, and much maligned. Although Asmodeus was originally an architect – he assisted in the building of Solomon's Temple – a geometer, mathematician, astronomer, and a teacher of the mechanical sciences, he later became the Persian and Hebrew personification of lust. In this form for example, Asmodeus was responsible for the drunkenness of Noah. Eventually he became a serpent. He can be invoked for help in finding anything under the ground.

Hermes – Hermes is the androgynous power, which connects and goes between the realms of Underworld, Middleworld and

Upperworld. Like Anubis, Hermes is the bringer of souls to the Underworld. He is the patron of travellers, and thieves. Like Thoth, Hermes is the inventor of astronomy, of the musical scale, of medicine, of weights and measures, of the alphabet, and of eloquence. He is thus the God of intellect, of communication, and of commerce – between all the worlds. The Staff of Hermes, the Caduceus, is the axis around which the cosmos turns. The Caduceus has two serpents coiled around it. They represent the balance of darkness and light, order and disorder, male and female – the polarities of life.

Hermes is the Roman Mercury, Quicksilver. The nature of which is ingenious, slippery and elusive. The mercury of the Alchemists had to become like the peacock with shimmering rainbow feathers. Hermes is the Phallic God, whose stones are rooted in the Underworld and reach up to the Heavens. From out of the darkness of earth and sky Hermes brings forth the many-coloured riches of creation. His animals are the cock, the ram and the tortoise. He is a thief, a trickster, the bringer of fertility, and of dreams. His child with Aphrodite, is Hermaphrodite, combining male and female.

5

God of Fertility

*The God is the lover of the Goddess. He brings the gleaming seed
into the womb-tomb of the Earth Mother on the darkest day of the
year, so renewing the cycle. He merges with the elements, crystallises
the liquid stone, makes patterns in the frozen water, vitalises the
dormant plants, and sustains the slumbering creatures. He
works within every living and non-living being upon the earth
to provide bones. From out of the primary source of the Mother
he distills the nourishment each thing needs to live.*

The God is a giver of wealth and fertility. The God is the God of
Life. The unfolding phenomena of life, the ceaseless coming into
being, the multiplicity and interpendence of all life forms, the sun
light, the waters, the earth, the trees, the creatures, the microbacteria
and the cells, are all the presence of the sacred in life. In the Hopi
tradition, Masau or Eototo, the God of Death and the Underworld,
is the beneficent God of Fertility. He is a protector, a guardian, and
the God whose inner fire causes crops to germinate and grow. He is
shown holding the corn plant. In the Semitic tradition, Baal is identified with the cycle of vegetative growth. He is the tree, the grain,
the harvest. In the Greek and Roman tradition, Dispater, Hades,
and Pluto are beneficent chthonian gods offering up the treasures
of the earth. Their names mean 'riches' or 'wealth-giver.' They are
the giver of crops, of minerals, and were honoured at all exception-
ally abundant fields, orchards, and springs.

Osiris, as an early Nile God, is the bestower of fertility. As the
God who dies and is reborn – like the seeds pressed into the
annual deposit of river mud – Osiris is the Bearer of Grain. His

recumbent body is portrayed with stalks of grain growing from it. Then, as the stalks are cut down, they produce the food that nourishes the people. Osiris may be seen in the context of the Near Eastern Dying and Rising Gods, whose lives embody the seasonal fertility cycle of the year.

The cults of Adonis, Tammuz, Attis, and Dumuzi, describe a cycle where the God alternates between half the year in the Upperworld and half the year in the Underworld. These Near Eastern gods die and are reborn with the harvest. They are rising, even as they fall. They imitate the lunar cycle of regeneration. They are all represented by a tree. They have a partner, a Mother Goddess, who either rescues them from the Underworld or, as in the case of Dumuzi, they rescue her from the Underworld. In such later cases as Hades or Dispater, they take her with them into the Underworld. They may take on an animal form as companion to the Goddess. The Dying and Rising God is the personification of the many forms of life undergoing the cycle of death and rebirth in nature – the realm of the Goddess.

In connection with his role beside the Goddess as augmenter of fertility, the God is highly sexual. He is strong and muscular. He often has a serpentine or a phallic character. The snakes that appear with the goddesses of the Neolithic era probably represent the male god. Robin Hood or Red Robin Hood is highly virile and phallic. Shiva, the third partner of the Hindu Trinity – the Destroyer, alongside the Creator, Brahma, and the Sustainer, Vishnu – is the classic example of the Phallic God. He is represented by the Lingam. Shiva is also the Lord of Death, dangerous, grim, and lethal. His love-making dance with the Death Goddess Kali brings the cosmos to the point of total annihilation. And, at that point, there can only be renewal. In sexual surrender to the Goddess Kali, Shiva becomes the death of death.

Geb or Seb, the Egyptian Earth God, is represented as lying on his back, forming the earth and mountains. His enormous penis reaches up to impregnate the over-arching Sky Goddess, Nut. The epiphanies of the highly sexual Greek God Dionysos, reveal him leading wildness, dance, frenzy, and total abandonment, to the point of his own dismemberment and annihilation. Then, from the point of no return – that is, from a place beyond the limits of the self – comes purification and rebirth.

Cernunnos – The Celtic Horned God of the Underworld and Fertility. The ancient Stag God. Little is recorded about Cernunnos, but from his representations among the Celts and the Provincial Romans who adopted him, he is a powerful chthonian God of Wealth and a Lord of the Animals. His constant animal companions are the bull, the stag and the ram-horned serpent – the chthonic provider and guardian of wealth. In his classic representation on the 1st Century B.C.E. Gundestrup Cauldron, Cernunnos is shown sitting erect and cross-legged. Antlers and leaves sprout from his head. He wears a torc around his neck and grasps another torc in his left hand. He holds a serpent in his right hand. Animals gather about him, including the ram-headed serpent. Other representations show Cernunnos with a full purse, or a stream of coins flowing from his lap.

Cernunnos is a benevolent God of the Underworld whose aid can be invoked for success in agricultural, commercial, sexual, or hunting activities. His abundance is in the trees and plants, the game, the herds, in offspring, or in the inspiration that flows from out of the head of a man who brings his inner nature into a dynamic balance. The balance of masculine and feminine is one of the meanings of the torc. 'Kern' means the crown of the head. Cernunnos is likely to mean the 'horned one.'

In his original form as a shape-shifter, Cernunnos is the guiding spirit of shamans. In the spring when his Underworld powers begin to wane, Cernunnos changes into an aspect known as Esus. After the flourishing of the trees, Esus is represented as a wood cutter. Esus gives way to Cernunnos as Stag King – the Lord of the Waning Year – in the fall. Cernunnos grasps the fecund but fiery power of the realm of earth. He sits at the dark root of the Tree of Life. He is the virile God who knows how to raise the serpent power, and transform it in the service of life and the Goddess.

Herne the Hunter – A late name for the Celtic Horned God of the Hunt and the Underworld. An oak cult celebrated Herne in

Windsor Forest. Herne is a descendent of Cernunnos. Herne is cognate to Cerne (plus suffix), in the Gaelic of Gaul, where the C, like the H, is pronounced 'ch.'

Dis, Dispater – 'Riches Father.' Roman and Gallic God of Death and the Underworld. A chthonic deity of fertility, but also a source of dis-ease. Husband of Prosperina. Occasionally depicted with a wolf head.

original form of payment will be issued for new and unread books and unopened music within 14 days from any Barnes & Noble store. For merchandise purchased with a check, a store credit will be issued. **Without an original receipt**, a store credit issued by mail will be offered at the lowest selling price. With a receipt, returns of new and unread books and unopened music from bn.com can be made for store credit. A gift receipt or exchange receipt serves as proof of purchase only.

Valid photo ID required for all returns, exchanges and to receive and redeem store credit. With a receipt, a full refund in the original form of payment will be issued for new and unread books and unopened music within 14 days from any Barnes & Noble store. For merchandise purchased with a check, a store credit will be issued. **Without an original receipt**, a store credit issued by mail will be offered at the lowest selling price. With a receipt, returns of new and unread books and unopened music from bn.com can be made for store credit. A gift receipt or exchange receipt serves as proof of purchase only.

Valid photo ID required for all returns, exchanges and to receive and redeem store credit. With a receipt, a full refund in the original form of payment will be issued for new and unread books and unopened music within 14 days from any Barnes & Noble store. For merchandise purchased with a check, a store credit will be issued. **Without an original receipt**, a store credit issued by mail will be offered at the lowest selling price. With a receipt, returns of new and unread books and unopened music from bn.com can be made for store credit. A gift receipt or excha...

6

Protector of Animals and Guardian of Nature

The God is the Guardian of Nature and the Protector of the Animals. He is the defender of their right to be sovereign and autonomous over themselves. He is the stag, rising and falling with the thrust of horns from the temples. His test of strength and velvet scent calls the fertile does. He is the Great Bear God, Artos. He is the Hound of Darkness, Cerberus. He is Cernunnos, the Stag King. He is the Fecund Bull, Dionysos. He is Robin Good-fellow, the Wild Herdsman – Gruagach, Bachlach, and Fachan.

The symbols of the God that correspond most closely to his fertility-enhancing and sexual attributes regularly manifest in theriomorphic or zoomorphic form, that is, in animal form. His most common animal forms are the wolf, the boar, the bull, the stag, serpent, and goat, although he has many others. Compared to the many depictions of the Goddess in Palaeolithic and Neolithic art, his relative absence is made up by the presence of very obviously male animals. These animals are often horned.

The ancient Greek and Roman God Pan is half-human and half-goat. The main attribute of Pan is his virility. Dionysos appeared annually as a bull to mate with a woman. This may represent the earliest form of Dionysos, and historians believe he is very old indeed. The Stag King appears annually in northern Europe to mate with the May Queen. Robin Hood, an ancient British God, is both bird and stag. He eventually became the defender of the wild wood and its animals against encroachment by church and civil authorities. Shiva is the snake and Lord of the Animals. He is the hunter, and the lover clad in the skins of wild animals.

As Protector of Animals the God is a universal deity who is some-times – especially in the Americas – their creator. He punishes those who abuse the wild creatures. He is called upon to guide the hunt and demands thanks for its successful conclusion. As their Guardian he dwells with the animals in the forest. He sometimes has the character of a tree, or shares attributes with the animals. He is part bull, bear, stag, leopard or lion. They emerge from, or are one with his body.

Representations from the Palaeolithic age attest to the Protector of Animals being among the earliest known roles of the God. The shamans painted in the Ice Age caves dancing in animal skins and horns, provide evidence that union with the animals was considered magic of the highest order. The paintings of bulls, mammoths, aurochs, rhinoceros, and stallions seem to be saying that if only their power could be harnessed – if only it could be felt – then the strength and abundance of the animals would surely come to the tribe. The act of painting a powerful animal was an act of vision and of sympathetic magic. The first discernible men in Palaeolithic art are always partly hidden in animal skins. The later Cernunnos, Dionysos, Pan, the Minotaur, are horned, cloven footed, shaggy. They mate or merge with a bull or another horned creature in some way. The deities that die on the lunar horns or tusks of animals suggest another aspect of the connection to this power. Their death is a sacrifice to life.

As the Neolithic cultures emerge into the historical record with their ubiquitous depictions of the agricultural Goddess – as fecund, rounded, buxom, female forms – the representations of the God, rather than of men, tend to remain zoomorphic. The Gods' epipha-nies as bull, serpent, stag, boar and lion, mean he continues to mate with the increasingly urban and culture-creating Goddess as the force of wild, untamed Nature. The mighty horned bull that appears in many Neolithic sacred contexts, such as the temples of Crete and Anatolia, although clearly associated with Goddess worship, cannot solely have signified the Goddess. The bull's heads – bucrania – that adorn the early temples of Çatal Hüyük in Anatolia, and Sardinia for example, are the sole manifestations of male energy in a context otherwise almost exclusively reserved for the feminine.

32

The horns of the God – of Set, Thoth, Herne, Cernunnos, Shiva, Pan, Loki, Baal, Dionysos, and others – are the outward sign of his inner transformational power. When Moses came down from the mountain after his encounter with the divine, it is said he bore horns – a relic from the old religion that the new studiously tried to avoid. When Cuchulainn enters his divine madness, a horn springs from his forehead. As the greatest hero of the Irish tradition, Cuchulainn exemplifies the true role of the warrior. He is the protector of the weak and the horned Guardian of Nature.

Like the moon, horns are lustrous, crescent-shaped, of the dark, and, when annual, they are waxing and waning. When permanent and conjoined, as in the mythical unicorn, they are said to be the power of pure spirit, clearing away obfuscation and dispelling poison. Any who have tried wearing horns know they require balance; they are the equilibrium of the rising and falling aspects of the God. As they grow each year, horns are the outer equivalent of the inner womb. When they shed their blood-rich velvet, the man is fully born. Horns are the epiphany of male power, which, rising and falling as spiral and crescent, are the perfect expression of the cycle that brings a man into harmony with the pervasive creative power of the feminine.

Gruagach – The British Wild Herdsman. The Gruagach is often seen as a powerful, capricious, but on the whole benevolent ruler of the Realm of Faery. The Gruagach is the Protector of the Animals and Guardian of Nature. He is sometimes seen possessing the single eye, arm and foot, characteristic of the Fachan. He is wild, but he directs the creative energies of nature. The aid of the Gruagach is invoked for pastoral and other work around the farm, but like other Brownies, he will be upset if clothes are left out for him as a reward.

Robin Hood – Robin Goodfellow, Robin of the Greenwood, or 'Red Robin Hood' after his tumescent phallus, is the popular defender of the Native British Tradition. He is the 'Good Man' who maintains the wild wood. He protects it against encroachment so that it will remain a sanctuary for those persecuted by authority and religion. Robin rights the wrongs inflicted upon the upholders of the ancient ways by the Church. He is the God of the Witches. As the Cock Robin slain in mid-winter, he is the Dying and Rising God. The red breast is his blood. Robin Hood is the Horned Stag or Reindeer Shaman willing to go into the freezing depths of the wintry earth to retrieve the riches that lie there. He gives those riches to everyone in his red-coated form of Father Christmas, drawn in his sleigh by reindeer.

The 'Hood' or the 'Hud' is the Yule log in which the spirit of the Lord of the Forest resides. It is the sacred pillar around which the rites of Mari-Anna, the Great Mother of the Grove, are performed. With the turn of winter over the solstice and the shedding of the blood of Red Robin, the Earth Goddess is renewed in her Maiden aspect. At Beltane, May Day, the rites are consummated, and greenwood marriages under the auspices of the renegade Friar Tuck performed. Robin, as the 'Archer of Love,' never misses a heart. Despite all opponents and any weather, Robin Hood, Maid Marian – the God and Goddess – and their coven of twelve 'Merry Men' continue to live in the sacred forest celebrating the rites that turn the Wheel of the Year.

Robin in French means 'ram' or 'devil.' Phallic or redheaded flowers tend to be given his name.

Bachlach – The club-carrying Irish Wild Herdsman. Precursor to the Green Knight of Arthurian Legend, the Bachlach challenges the heroes of Ireland to a beheading game. His head always returns intact to his shoulders. Only Cuchulainn dare present his neck for the return stroke. The test of courage passed, the Bachlach reveals himself as Cu Roi Mac Daire, a Lord of the Underworld. Cu Roi is the shape-shifting challenger and guardian on the path of knowledge. He is the keeper of the entrance to the Underworld, described as a revolving castle or a grassy mound. The Bachlach is an elemental being, similar to the Fachan and Gruagach.

Fachan – The club-carrying Scottish Wild Herdsman. A one-legged, one-eyed, one-armed, shaggy, or leaf clad giant of the North. The Protector of the Animals. Perhaps part animal himself, the Fachan is the guardian of the entrance to the Underworld.

7

Lover

The God is the Sacred King who goes down into the Underworld seeking his bride, the Goddess. He enters her furrow, performs the Sacred Marriage in the bed of last year's leaves. He is torn apart and dismembered by her libidinous madness. He dies to himself in her so that he may be reborn in her. He re-enters the Underworld and is grieved, sought for and restored by her. He sprouts upward, coming and going within her body. He is the Lord of the Cycle of Death and Resurrection. He is Bel, Attis, Baal, Orpheus, Osiris, Dumuzi, Adonis and Arthur.

The God is a lover. He loves and is loved by the Goddess. At the heart of all mythology is a love story, where the God seeks and enters the ultimate chamber of the Goddess and their union creates new life. The love affair of Isis and Osiris is among the greatest of all time. She longs for, and restores his body every year. Adonis is deeply loved by two Goddesses, Aphrodite – the Goddess of Love herself – and Persephone, Queen of the Underworld. Tammuz is the lover of Ishtar; Attis the lover of Cybele; and Baal the lover of Anat. Dumuzi is the lover of Inanna. In one version of the Sumerian myth of Inanna, Dumuzi gives himself up to the Underworld so she may return.

The Gods of the Underworld also have partners: Hades and Persephone, Dispater and Prosperina, Gwynn and Creiddylad, Pwyll and Rhiannon, Shiva and Kali. They are responsible for earthly fertility, and it is frequently the case that they are also brother and sister. Originally the Goddess took their twin, the Sky God, as a lover, but with the ascendancy of patriarchy, this God usually became her destroyer. Then the hero or the son of the Sky God goes into and destroys the Underworld and its Gods. Apollo, for example, slays the Python, Beowulf slays Wendel. The more recent in time, the greater is the tendency for unequal patriarchal social patterns to dominate, and for the God to be an all powerful light and sky god, who deals out destruction on ever punier gods and goddesses of fertility and nature. The further we go back in time, the greater the tendency for the Goddess to become the more pervasive figure, for matricentric social patterns to predominate – such as brother-sister authority and endogamous marriage – for the God to be a god of nature and the animals, and for there to be equality between men and women.

It is important to state here that unlike the Judaeo-Christian and Islamic concept of God, the ancient mythic God is rarely seen as a creator, even when he is a God of Fertility. Creation may lie in the union of God and Goddess, but there is nothing to suggest in pagan tradition that the God has omnipotent or life-giving powers. Where the God is seen as a creator, it is when the plants and the animals are a part of, or emanate from, his body. He is not separate from the creation. In him the creation is revealed. This is a complete reversal of the prevailing view. If the Goddess is seen as the supreme metaphor for Nature itself, life-creating and life-taking, then the God is the metaphor for the life-energy that undergoes those transformations. He is at the effect of birth, life and death. He is the suppliant to life, or the protector of it. He is the living and dying aspect of her whole. Osiris is the classic example of this. Osiris represents the soul experiencing every aspect of existence.

In some traditions, the God increases and augments the flow of life-energy around the cycle of death and regeneration by virtue of the activities of men at particular places and times. While the Australian Aborigines for example, understand very well that a child is not conceived or born without sexual intercourse, the importance of sex lies in the man 'opening a doorway' for the spirit of the child to enter the creative matrix of the womb. Of course there is little way of knowing what the spiritual views of the early Europeans were, but it is to ideas like those of the Aborigines – especially where are correlations of art and material culture – that we can look for understanding and interpretation.

The partnerships formed by the archetypal images of the Gods and Goddesses provide the symbolic language for the understanding of and the acting out of our own relationships. In our early maturity we may act out the passionate love affairs of the underworld fertility Gods, but perhaps find ourselves still under the influence of our parents, returning home for part of the year. In our adult parenting phase the images of the home-making, hearth-centred, agricultural earth gods and goddesses may provide meaning. In our maturity we may form relationships on the basis of the wise, co-creating archetypal divine imagery. And of course, we may always seek the universal partner, who as god to goddess, goddess to god, god to god, or goddess to goddess, enables us to fulfill our greatest potentials.

The dance of love between partners in life is the model for the dance of love we do with life on earth, and that in turn is the model for the dance we do with the infinite. The steps of one imitate and teach us the dance we do with the other. The dance of God and Goddess expresses our deepest longings, aspirations and passions. Whether modelled for us on the cinema screen, on the pages of a novel, in the images of our faith, or in the moments of love we share with another, to imagine this dance enacted out in the infinity of the cosmos by divine lovers is to arrive among the most sublime possibilities our existence offers. Our deepest longing is discovered in the dance of God or Goddess as symbols of the flow of life on earth and as symbols of the infinite aspects of our soul as lover and beloved.

Adonis – A Semitic and Classical God of seasonal fertility, vegetation and rebirth. Adonis is born from a trunk of a tree. He alternates between the summer months as lover of the beautiful Aphrodite (originally Astarte) and the winter months in the Underworld as lover of Persephone. He has four months off every year in-between. His rites begin in spring and end after the harvest. Then women mourn for him and his beauty. Adonis is the God who dies to be reborn. He is like the seed that gives itself to the earth and so transforms into new life. Eventually Adonis was cut down – in a field of lettuce – by being gored in "the thigh" by a boar.

Some say Ares did the deed on the instigation of a jealous Aphrodite. But the act is in the time-honored pattern of the myth cycle of the God. He dies and rises as the son and lover of the Great Goddess. A similar fate met Osiris, Tammuz, and the Irish Diarmuid, all lovers of the Goddess. The centre of the cult of Adonis was the ancient sanctuary of Byblos on the east coast of the Mediterranean. This is where the Goddess Isis found Osiris in an Erica tree.

Attis – A Dying and Rising God of vegetation and herds, similar to Adonis. Unlike Adonis he castrates himself with a flint sickle; some say for being divided in love between the Goddess and a mortal woman. But like Adonis, at least in the older Lydian version of his myth, he is slain on the lunar tusks of a boar. Attis is the consort of the Earth Goddess Cybele. Their ecstatic rites are practiced at the spring equinox. Attis, or Endymion, probably originated as a Phrygian Tree God to whom the pine is sacred.

Dumuzi – Southern Sumerian God of Vegetation and the Underworld. He is equivalent to the northern Sumerian Tammuz. One tradition has Dumuzi, the 'Loyal Son,' spending half the year in the Underworld and half the year in the realm of the living. He takes the place of his mother, sister and lover, the Goddess Inanna, in the Underworld. His sister Geshtinanna takes his place when he returns bringing fertility with him. Another tradition does not have Dumuzi returning – the price paid for the restoration of Inanna. To ensure the continuation of seasonal fertility the Kings of Uruk became Dumuzi and ritually mated with Inanna represented by a priestess. Dumuzi is the God of the Sacred Marriage. Sometimes he is represented as a bull, sometimes as a mere child. He is the divine shepherd and was personified by the huge bud of the date palm.

8

Shape-Shifter

The God is the guide to the shadow side of the self. He is the truth that is never spoken in company. Before him all are exposed as profound and shallow, loving and envious, high and low, brave and cowardly. He guides the journey through the dark emotions, the primeval, reptilian forest, the dank roots of decay. He is the seer, the protector, the judge, and the measure of the fullness of the soul. He is the Wolf God Wepwawet, Sukunyum, Yama, Masau, Jizo, Anubis, Erebus and Hades.

The origin of the zoomorphic symbolism of the God may lie in the once widespread practice of shamanism. From comparison with surviving shamanistic cultures the case for a native European shamanic tradition reaching back into the Palaeolithic is a fairly easy one to make. The, at least 13,000 years old, animal-skinned and horned dancer in the cave of Trois Fréres for example, finds his equivalent in the practices of contemporary shamans.

Through the donning of the skin and horns of an animal a magic can be wrought that ensures health and fertility. It is through communion with the animal that the hunter knows where to seek them. A pact is established between the hunter and the hunted before a kill can be made. In the Medieval period the main charge levelled at men by the Inquisition was that of shape shifting, specifically into the form of a wolf. Women were more commonly accused of witchcraft. In the few cases where the whole charge was not a prefabricated Christian construct – a pact with the Devil and so on – the records say the accused spoke of visions, of flying through the air, entering the Underworld, and struggling with those forces that brought sickness and opposed fertility. All these things are characteristic of shamanic practice. This suggests, if not a remaining, then at least a vestigial shamanic tradition at this time.

The wolf features in several traditions of the God and has an extremely early, special relationship to humanity. The observation and the emulation of the hunting techniques of wolves and then their domestication, mean that wolves figure hugely in the rites of hunter-gatherers. Together, the human and the hound made a formidable team capable of journeying successfully almost anywhere. The Egyptian wolf headed God Wepwawet, was the "opener of the trails" to the Underworld. Wepwawet guides the boat of Ra. The warriors of Odin, the 'beserkers,' wore wolf-skins in their search for the ecstasy that brought extra-sensory perception and invulnerability in war. Wolf-clans, wolf-shamans, wolf-brother-hoods – such as that of Odin – were widespread in the ancient world. As a strong pagan tradition surviving into medieval times, the wolf received the same treatment as the Horned God. The wolf became diabolic. Anyone who showed a sign of shamanistic practice, such as vision seeking through the aid of a power animal, was accused of being a werewolf.

Afagddu – The hideously ugly son of the Celtic Goddess Cerridwen. It was for Afagddu, 'utter darkness,' that Cerridwen prepared her Cauldron of Knowledge and Inspiration. He is the rightful recipient of the brew but it is taken from him by the youth Gwion. As a result, the Goddess pursues Gwion. He changes form into animals. Eventually he is caught as a speck of grain on the threshing floor of the Goddess. She assumes the form of a Hen, swallows him, and after nine months he is reborn as the poet Taliesin – 'radiant browed.' It may be that Afagddu-Gwion-Taliesin is one person, undergoing a three-stage initiatory transformation.

Odin – The Scandinavian and German deities divide into two main groups, one early in time and one later. The earlier deities, such as Freyr and Freyja, are known as the Vanir and appear as chthonian gods and goddesses of fertility. The later deities originate in the male-dominated, sky-oriented, Indo-European pantheon. These deities, the Aesir, are more well known, demand battle and sacrifice and include Odin in their number. They assume many of the attributes of the Vanir. The God Odin, Wotan or Woden, is the Lord of Death and the Underworld. He appears to have many of Freyr's attributes but is also a Sky God. He is the ruler of magic and language, the journeyer between the worlds. Odin's name is connected to words that mean spirit, wind, inspiration, ecstasy, fury, possession and madness. His is the power of speech through the breath. Like Hermes he is able to change shape and move like the wind between the worlds.

Odin underwent the ordeal of being hung on the World Tree, Yggdrasil, for nine nights to gain wisdom. He made the offering of "myself to my self." He returned with the gift of the runes – a symbol alphabet or language – for humanity. The runes are primarily for divination. Odin gave up an eye to drink of the Well of Wisdom and Remembrance that lies at the foot of the tree. His bird is the raven, his animal the wolf. He becomes an eagle in order to see all the worlds or to gather up the dead for the spirit world. He rides with the horsemen of the Wild Hunt on his eight-legged horse Sleipnir. He is the terrible god of battle, of warriors and carries a spear. He presides over the 'beserkers' – those who fought naked or with only the skin of the wolf (or bear) for protection. Odin is the half-brother of Loki, and father of Balder, Tyr and Thor.

Wepwawet – The Egyptian Wolf-headed God. God of the Underworld and the "opener of roads." Wepwawet guides the dead and the boat of Ra through the Underworld. He is the leader of processions, the Lord of the Necropolis, and is usually dressed and ready for war.

9

God of the Tree

The God is the pine, the holly, the cedar, fir and yew. He is the tree that flourishes in the dark forest and grows in the dark half of the year. He is the tree with needles, thorns and toxic berries, whose wood makes weapons of death. He is the ivy, mushroom and toadstool, the plants that thrive on decay. He is Tammuz, the Green Man, and Robin of the Greenwood, the Lord of the Forest.

The God may manifest as a tree, or in some other green and leafy form. He may appear in the act of emerging from a tree, or from a grass-covered mound. Adonis is born from a tree. Osiris is reborn from a tree. Dumuzi is the date palm. Tammuz is the pine. The latter two are the Sumerian 'Lords of the Tree of Life.' Baal guards the cedar, the Canaanite Tree of Life. In the Underworld, Dionysos is identified with Okeanos, a primordial foliate God of vegetation. The Celtic Cernunnos is shown sprouting leaves. Robin Hood dwells in the forest. Folk traditions of Robin Hood and the Wild Man preserve aspects of the lore surrounding the Dying and Rising God of Vegetation. The precursor of the Green Knight, the Bachlach, dwells in the wilds. No matter how often he is cut down, usually in a beheading game, he always rejuvenates in the manner of a tree.

These features of the God are consistent with his role as the God of Fertility within an annual cycle of the death and rebirth of vegetation. Representations of this aspect of the God suggest this role came later than his role as Guardian of Animals – that is, it came about during the period of the emergence of agriculture. The tree however, as the image of the *axis mundi,* the world axis or ladder on which the shaman journeys between the worlds, is likely to lie deep in the stratigraphy of the human collective unconsciousness. Odin hangs on the World Tree Yggdrasil to gain his wisdom. He journeys to the roots of the Underworld and drinks of the Well of Remembrance that lies there. A similar journey is implied for Osiris as a result of his death and 'resurrection' within a tree. He goes from the depths to the heights.

Although obscured, a tree plays a commanding role in early Judaic and Christian mythology. The Tree of Life is an ancient and universal symbol of the divine power immanent in the world. The serpent is the symbol of this power. Early Sumerian engraved seals depict the Tree of Life with the Goddess and her serpent on one side and the Horned God on the other.

Dreams and visions of the cutting down or the destruction of a tree or a forest, run deep into the collective unconsciousness as symbols of the loss of the sacred. They signify our deepest fears over the loss of life. A burnt and denuded treeless world is a symbol of ultimate loss. They represent the fear that the God may not rise again if the destruction of life is too great.

Tammuz – Mesopotamian God of Vegetation and Fertility. The equivalent of Dumuzi. Each year Tammuz is rescued by his lover, the Goddess Ishtar, from the Underworld. In summer, after the harvest, the rites of mourning for Tammuz begin. Originally a Tree God, Tammuz is the representation of the cycle of life and death in nature. He rises from the earth in spring, performs the rites of sacred marriage with the Mother or Earth Goddess, and returns to the earth in autumn. All the rituals of the Dying and Rising Gods, of Adonis, Attis, Baal and Dumuzi, include dramatic re-enactments of their annual cycle of life: sacred marriage, death and resurrection.

Green Man – A Northern European deity of vegetation. He is usually shown as just a head with leaves pouring from his mouth, or, less frequently, from his eyes, ears, cheeks and nose. The Green Man is the personification of the fertility and wealth of the cycle of life throughout the year. As the Celts saw the trees as the embodiment of wisdom and the provider of letters and language, it is possible to view the Green Man as the power that connects the head – that is, the intelligence – of a man to the chthonian power of the earth. This power is then expressed from the head, through the mouth, in poetry, song, recantation, satire, or any of the verbal arts. The Green Man insists the words of men remain true to life. He serves as a reminder to men where their wisdom springs from. The Green Man is related to the Wild Man and, as the Bachlach, his constant quest to keep men "true to their word" will result in the loss of their heads if they fail.

In the Classical tradition, the Green Man is related to an early foliate aspect of Dionysos-Bacchus called Okeanos, and later known as Silvanus. He is an ancient chthonian God as there is no doubt where his power comes from. In Egypt, green is the colour of life, and Osiris is sometimes shown with a green head.

10

The God as *Axis Mundi*

The God is the centre of life. He is the end of thought. He is the ground of every ending and every beginning. The world turns around him, but he is at rest. In his above and in his below the stars and precious stones gleam with iridescent colours. Without his radius they would be lost. The God is the sacred mountain, the staff, the herm, the pillar, and the sacred tree joining the Underworld, the Middleworld and the Upperworld.

Although he is not a creator, the God knows his way through the world. He knows its centre, its axis, its edges, and its directions. In mythology there are many descriptions of the God impressing his body into the earth, of becoming a pillar, or hanging upon the world tree. Llew is suspended in the ash tree seeking healing and restoration. Odin hangs upon Yggdrasil seeking the wisdom of the runes. Christ is suspended upon a cross. Diarmuid, as Summer King, hides in the branches of the world tree from Finn the Winter King, who waits at its foot. At stake is the passage of Grainne, the Solar Goddess, through her cycle of the year.

The God shows the way through the Tree of Life and Knowledge to gain access to all realms. The God is the lightning flash cutting through the formless chaos of the storm. He knows what it means to give himself up to the powerful core of the universe, and there be renewed by its fundamental order.

The God as gnomon brings order to the chaos of nature. The staff of the surveyor planted in the ground, aligned to sun, moon and stars, and thus to the calendar and to time, is the primary act of order. The act establishes the centre, the place of origin. The

45

centre is the place of power and the symbolic focus of unity. From the centre emerges order and thus government. It is also the point upon the apparent plane of the earth's surface that possesses a vertical dimension. This connects the centre to heaven and to the underworld, to the above and to the below. A fissure or a cave, a tree, a mound or mountain, a stone or some other pillar set in the ground and reaching to the above, may represent this. The marker at the centre is the *gnomon,* the *omphalos*, the world navel, and around it lies the circumference. The circumference – which need not be round, and indeed is often square – marks the *temenos*. This is the boundary between the primal ground of unity within and the differentiated ground without. The Greek word temenos is closely related to the Latin words for 'temple,' 'template' and 'time.' The gnomon not only provides the measure for defining sacred space but for defining time.

Over the course of history, the God as the simple stick stuck in the ground to delineate the order of a camp, became the stone monument at the centre of the seats of governments. The 555 feet 6 inch tall (6,666 inches) obelisk, the Washington Monument, in the capital of the United States is a classic example. The geometry and numerology of its design is an expression of national power. The danger here of course is of the order created by the centre becoming too rigid and totalitarian. With the rise of the secular state, the symbolic and sacred component of the gnomon has become lost, and the emphasis has fallen upon upholding the state and its established economic, social, religious and political systems at any cost. The God must rise and fall however, and we find in the ancient traditions of the Gods the wisdom to avoid such excessive centralisation of power.

The God suspended upon the world tree for example, dying and finding resurrection through its annual cycle of growth, is fundamental to the mysteries of the Gods of the Near East. Dumuzi, the date palm, gives himself up to the depths of the Underworld to rescue Ianna. He rises and falls in step with the annual cycle of fertility in the desert lands. Osiris rises and dies with the fertility provided by the Nile. The death and resurrection of Christ, his mystics claim, is central to the renewal of creation itself. The God as the divine pillar, the phallus, the lingam, the cross, even and especially in his death, provides men with an exemplary model not only for the architectural order of their world but also for their conduct within it.

Atlas – The Titan Atlas, brother of Prometheus, separated the waters of the firmament from the waters of the earth during the time of creation. Said to be the founder of Atlantis, and the keeper of the apples in the Garden of the Hesperides, Atlas bears the celestial sphere upon his shoulders.

Astraios – The Greek God or Titan of the Night Sky. Astraios, the "starry one," and his wife Eos, the dawn, conceived Phosphorus the morning star, as well as the North, South and West Winds.

Masau – The Hopi God of Death and the Underworld. As a Creator God at the "root of the world," Masau guided the people up from the previous worlds. In the present world, the Fourth World, Masau or Eototo is a benevolent God who guides and protects the people. He is a God of fertility, agriculture and fire. His heat causes crops to germinate and grow.

Geb – Geb, or Seb or Keb, is the Egyptian God of the Earth and the Underworld. After Ra separated him from his sister Nut, the Sky, his phallus rose up to continue joining with her. Together they produced Osiris, Isis, Set and Nephythys. Geb is also a God of tombs and vegetation.

11

The Destroyer and the Destroyed

The God is the Lord of Death and Compassion. All are made equal on his common ground of desire and death. The God makes the journey through winter, through the terrible night of the soul. His is the ecstasy of release, destruction, sacrifice and letting go. He is the Other, by whom wildness, madness and frenzy brings purification. He is Dionysos, Mara, Chernobog, Dis Pater, Set and Bhairab, the Lord of the Necropolis.

The God is the destroyer. He appears with an axe, a spear, a sickle, a sword, a club. Dionysos and his Maenads tear apart the body of their victims. They are the "eaters of raw flesh." Odin is the terrible god of battle. His wolf and bear beserkers are destruction personified. Shiva in general has this quality, but he also has aspects said to be even more destructive. This fierce form of Shiva is known as Bhairab in India, and in Bali as Kala. Kala is the Lord of Destruction who lives in the centre of the earth. In the Egyptian tradition, Set, the brother and slayer of Osiris, presides over storms, droughts, winds and the night. He is everything his brother is not. In his serpent form of Apep, Set fights to keep the sun in the Underworld. He destroys what his brother gives. Ultimately Set and Osiris – the giver of life – are one. Through death comes life.

A similar treatment of the Gods is found in the Nahuatl, or the Aztec tradition. Born of primordial darkness, the four Tezcatlipocas are the Gods of Heaven and the Underworld, of darkness and of light, as well as the cardinal directions. Black Tezcatlipoca of the north is the terrible Lord of Death and destruction, invoked in war. Red Tezcatlipoca of the east annually dies and is reborn as the God of Vegetation. The Tezcatlipoca of the west is Queztalcoatl. He is also a God of Night and the Underworld, but his realm is that of fecundity and life. In every case where these traditions are affected by monotheism, these deities are now morally equated with evil and shunned.

A consistent theme of the God is that he is also destroyed. In the story of Set and Osiris, Set has a sarcophagus made to the exact measurements of Osiris. Set then organises a banquet during which the sarcophagus is offered to whoever it fits exactly. When Osiris lies down within it, of course it is a perfect fit. Set and seventy-two companions rush forward, seal the coffin and throw it into the Nile. After the body of Osiris is found by Isis at Byblos, returned to Egypt, and concealed among the reeds of the Nile, Set assumes the form of a boar and tears it into fourteen pieces.

The Death Goddess Cerridwen devours Gwion, as a grain of wheat, in the Celtic tradition. The Celtic Bran is decapitated, as is Shiva. The Wild Herdsman, the Bachlach, the Green Knight, and the Green Man are also decapitated. Adonis, Attis, Diarmuid and the other alternating Gods, are gored to death by a boar. The monstrous serpent Mot destroys Baal. The Barley God and the other grain deities are cut down, parched, then ground to pieces. Dionysos is torn apart by the celebrants of his mysteries. In the Orphic tradition, Dionysos is dismembered and scattered in seven pieces by the Titans. The God must die for there to be rebirth.

Dismemberment of a corpse figures strongly in the ancient traditions. A common form of Neolithic burial practice was to leave the body out – exhumation – to be defleshed either by humans or animals, or to disinter it after a period of time underground. The bones were then arranged within a collective ossuary such as a megalithic passage mound. The bones of the ancestors then might be taken out periodically, their rituals enacted, their stories told, before being returned to the world of the dead. The evidence for this practice is provided by passage mounds such as Newgrange in Ireland and West Kennet in Britain, where the nature, amount and the arrangement of the bones can be interpreted as ritual dismemberment.

In some traditions, the Creation itself is the body of a dismembered Giant. The dismembered body of the Scandinavian giant

Ymir, the Persian giant Gayomart, the Hindu giant Purusha, and the Chinese giant P'an Ku, forms the earth, the waters, the mountains, the sky, and even the heavenly bodies. In the traditions of the people of what is now central and northern Arizona, the God – the son of the first grandmother – presses his gigantic body into the earth. Each place in the landscape then possesses medicinal plants appropriate for healing that part of the body.

The division of the pieces of a body at a feast is a crucial issue in mythical literature and among contemporary tribal cultures. The best portions go to the king and queen, the next best to the champion, the blacksmith and the bard, and so on, until the remainder goes to the people. Some parts of the body belong to the spirits. Sharing in the consumption of a body is at once a statement about origins, the unity of the gathering, and the exact social place of each person who partakes in the meal. Sharing in the body of the God is a recreation of the order, the division and the unity of life. The eating of raw flesh in Dionysian frenzy seeks out an ecstatic experience of unity through the release of all inhibition. Articulating the body in a grave or long barrow makes a precise statement about the perceived order of life in relation to the realm of the ancestors. Consuming medicine grown on the heart of the God is the direct revelation of spirit in nature. The eating of consecrated bread representing the presence of the God is yet another response to this symbolic mystery.

Bhairab – The Indian and Nepalese Hindu God who represents the terrible aspect of Shiva. Bhairab is nude, and usually black or dark blue in colour. He has sixty-four forms, all of them fierce. He has skulls in his necklace, girdles and crown. He is attended by a dog, and is often shown dancing upon a recumbent figure. In his many arms he carries weapons. This destructive form of Shiva is known as Kala in Bali. Kala dwells at the centre of the earth.

Yama – Hindu and Buddhist God of the Underworld and Death. Despite his fierce representation with skulls and chopper, Yama is a benevolent deity whose task is to look after the well being of the dead. In the Vedic tradition he was the first man and thus the first person to die. He is 'the leveller' and impartial Judge of the Dead. He rides a black thunder horse and may be depicted with a bull's head.

Tezcatlipoca – Toltec God of War, the Night Sky, Death and the Underworld. He was adopted by the Aztecs and was also known by the Mayans. The many aspects of Tezcatlipoca mean he is also a God of Duality ruling both dark and light, heaven and hell, strife and prosperity. In the early Nahuatl cosmologies the Tezcatlipocas were four gods. They are born in the time of darkness and are called the 'Smoking Mirrors.' Red Tezcatlipoca or Xipe is a God of Death and Resurrection, living and dying, who is sacrificed with the seasonal cycle of the year. He dwells in the east. Black Tezcatlipoca is the Lord of Death, Destruction and the north. He is the patron of warriors and sorcerers. In his role as God of the storms, hurricanes and the night he is capricious rather than evil. He is the night jaguar. Blue Tezcatlipoca dwells in the south. The fourth God is Queztalcoatl, 'feathered serpent,' the God of Life and Fertility. His domain also lies in the night sky – in the west as the evening star and in the east as the morning star.

12

Trickster

The God is the fool, the risk taker, the adventurer into the unknown. His drumbeat passes between the villages, communicating unseen knowledge. He pushes the limits of the possible, and ameliorates his discoveries with buffoonery. His ridicule and laughter probe deeply, asking for each and every article of faith to be questioned and examined closely. He is Manannán, Mudhead, Loki, the Pied Piper, Coyote, the Trickster and the Satirist.

Among the common themes running through the universal traditions of the God is that of the trickster, magician, and fool. Loki, for example, entertains the Nordic pantheon. Although known as the God of wickedness and mischief he is not evil, but capricious and sociable. Loki is father to the wolf and to the serpent that wraps around the human realm of Midgard. In the Celtic Tradition, the wise God Manannán often appears as a clown. In this manner he deceives the pompous and the gullible and reveals secrets only to those open enough to hear them. Like the Father God the Daghda, Manannán is willing to play the fool to benefit humanity. His tricks range from mere pranks, apparently carried out in drunkenness that seem to turn back upon him, to profound revelations. The same can be said of the Trickster, Coyote, and the hunched-back flute player Kokopelli, in the Native American traditions.

In many places it is the act of the putting on the horns, the skins, or the mask of the God that provides the license to play the fool. Horn-wearing Satyrs introduced the Roman Saturnalia. In the Americas, the Kachina deities of the Pueblo cultures are always accompanied by masked clowns, who, in the case of the Hopi Mudheads, are Kachinas themselves. It is hard to imagine a clown cavorting down the aisles of a Protestant church during a Sunday service, but it is at equivalent ceremonies in the Native American tradition that the clowns appear, bursting the notion that the sacred and divine always have to be serious.

It is possible that Prometheus can be considered a God. A Titan of "the Time before time," Prometheus was so concerned for the welfare of humanity that he tricked Zeus by bringing many benefits, including fire, to the inhabitants of earth. The Titans, or the giants in general, love tricks and joke playing, and, as they are the *ge-antes* – 'the dwellers on the earth before' – they are held responsible for all the quirks and novelties, the strange and bizarre features of the landscape today.

The role of the God as Trickster is to stand outside the normal pattern of affairs and push the limits. The Saturnalia, ironically presided over by Saturn, the God of limits, deliberately broke social restrictions. It turned the classes upside down, and approved licentious sexual behaviour. In the Americas, those whose sexuality was ambiguous took the role of pushing the social limits. The man who was a woman, the woman who was a man, the person who did not fit into the social norms, had a role to play in getting society to not take itself too seriously. Dionysos, of course, with his ambivalent sexuality, was the God of sexual licence and abandonment. Everything he did turned the notion of normality upon its head. It is quite likely beneath the veneer placed upon the Gods, and especially among the Gods vanished from view altogether, there is an aspect that embodies everything contrary to the norm. Apart from the Tricksters and the Gods of the Underworld, some of the most likely candidates for this role are the Gods (and Goddesses) of homosexuality. Coyote, the Trickster God of North America for example, is always encouraging flirtations among the same sex.

It is difficult for those of us born in the Western world to grasp the playful aspect of the God. We are raised on theism of the most serious kind, and, as a result, project serious notions onto the very mention of God or Goddess. If for example, Roman writers refer to a provincial deity they identify with Mars or Juno, there is a tendency to assume that the deity carries the same weight that our culture, with its monotheistic and transcendent outlook, identifies with God. The local figure in question might be a deified ancestor, a local hero, possible even a sporting champion who went on to make huge contributions to his hometown and was given a monument and a shrine as a result. The same adulation that a boy gives his sporting hero, even the professed willingness to die for him or for what his team stands for, might provide a better measure for understanding much of what we read or dig up from the past, than the casting of it into the realm of 'ritual' or the 'gods.'

The trickster, the clown, the judge, the shape-shifter, the magician, the eternal youth, the psychopomp, the lover, the protector, the craftsman, the sportsman, the sage and the keeper of wisdom, are aspects of ourselves projected onto the great reflexive screen of the universe. It is here we call them aspects of the divine, sacred, and of the Gods. It is human nature to elevate or reify someone or something with a reality it does not really have; but it is important to remember we live in a world of real things which are always in change, so that all we create in our human world with our human minds will also change and fall away. The trickster is here to remind us that even or especially our gods will perish, that even apparently among the deepest, most eternal images of the divine, there is self-parody, mockery, transience, something outside the norm.

Loki – Originally a Scandinavian God of fire and the hearth, Loki slowly became associated with trickery and mischief. He is not all bad but a sociable spirit who causes misrule, bawdy and parody. Loki is father of the wolf, the cunning trailblazer. He is also the father of Odin's horse, Sleipnir, and of the serpent that encircles Midgard – the realm where humans live. He is a shape-shifter, often assuming the form of a fly. After he instigated the death of the Good God Balder, Loki hid from the Gods in the form of animals, including the salmon, the embodiment of wisdom. In some traditions Loki is the maker of a powerful sword. Christian writers made Loki into an evil spirit. They say he is bound in a deep cavern where his struggles shake the earth. He will eventually break free and initiate the great transformation of the last days.

Manannan Mac Lir – Celtic God of the Sea and the Otherworld. In Celtic mythography the sea is the path to the Underworld. In the *Voyage of Bran*, Manannán appears in his chariot upon the waves and points the way. A son of Llyr, and thus a brother of Bran, Manannán is one of the most powerful deities in the Celtic pantheon. God of Wisdom and Magic, Manannán made the Crane Bag of Secrets. Originally a primal Goddess, the crane is an otherworldly bird bringing sacred wisdom, poetry and language. Manannán is a shape-shifter and a changer of the elements. He is the keeper of supernatural swine. He causes his home the Isle of Man to be hidden from its enemies by the power of illusion. He can arrive unchallenged in the courts of kings disguised as a buffoon or a clown, to perform ridiculous tricks. After the death of Pwyll, Manannán married Rhiannon, Horse Goddess and Queen of the Underworld, but his first and possibly his true love was Fand, a Goddess of glamour, pleasure and healing. In the Otherworld Manannán presides over the 'Feast of Age.'

Saturn – The Roman name for the Greek God Cronos. The one major addition the Romans added to his veneration was the Saturnalia. This was a period of misrule, around the end of the year (December 17–23), when all social constraints were overturned. This was viewed as a healthy renewal and a return to the original state of nature.

13

Craftsman

The God is the patron of smiths and miners. He lies in the depths of the earth guiding them to its riches. He mines the depths of the sensuous earth mother to bring forth life. Through application of hissing and spitting fire, he turns metal into weapons, tools, and ornaments. He is the fine, shining crystalline structure bringing order to the amorphic chaos of earth and sky. He is Goibniu, Govannon, Wayland, Hephaistos, Vulcan.

As the various symbolic aspects of the God are developed in this book, one of the difficulties is the lack of evidence from the important source of prehistory. Prehistory may be defined by a line drawn between societies that wrote and those that did not. Lacking the written word, about all we have left is archaeological material, and with just that evidence there is a huge problem of interpretation. We may have an artefact, a picture, something solid and material, but we don't have anyone writing about it to tell us what it means. What is a high status object in one region, may be a child's toy in another.

The prehistorical Agricultural Revolution was a critical turning point in the nature of the God, and a huge shift for men. The technology that made hunting obsolete and urban settlement, agriculture and pastoralism possible is archaeologically retrievable, but we know little from the material evidence about the psychological impact of the changes. One of the issues is that archaeology has necessarily focused on the retrievable. It is much easier to excavate and understand an urban centre than it is to even find an area where animals were herded for example, or trading activities took place, or outdoor ritual practiced. And it is here that we find a dividing line between men and women. It is easier to find the early urban centres of civilisation where mostly women's activities took place than it is to find the rural locations where mostly men's activities took place. We can find the pots, looms, fire pits, and ovens in the fixed and permanent dwellings of the women, but we cannot find the drying racks, the fireplaces, the corrals, the travelling forges, and the craft workshops of the more mobile men.

Another issue is that for several decades it has been popular to argue the evidence from the early, say 7th to 4th millennium B.C.E., urban centres around the Mediterranean and the Black Sea, indicated a matrifocal, goddess worshipping, and essentially peaceful society. It may be true, but this interpretation was possible because only the urban centres were excavated, leaving the activities of men on the sea shore, river bank, in the woods, mines, and groves largely untouched. The activities of men in these societies were peripheral to the easily excavatable urban centres, but not peripheral in social, economic, and spiritual significance. We can imagine that rites developed into established traditions over thousands of years were maintained by men who preferred to practice them outdoors, away from habitation. This is certainly the case today among men in tribal circumstances today. Men's and women's activities and circles take place in very different locations. Although we may know less about the men and the God of prehistory than we do of the women and the Goddess, his rites as craftsman, farmer, pastoralist, hunter, blacksmith, storyteller, mythmaker, musician, and initiator went on, and were deeply important to the life of society.

With the prevalence of Goddess focussed ideology in popular historical interpretation, and with the prevailing deeply entrenched notions of theism – belief in an external creator God – it is doubly difficult to develop an accurate idea of the progress of the God in Western history. It is hard to track him on the basis of the evidence alone through prehistory, through the Agricultural Revolution, through the ascendency of monotheism, and now into industrial and post-modern times. Yet it is the aspect of the God as craftsman that is especially helpful to our understanding. The technological creativity of the human world easily projects itself onto the screen

Table 2. Aspects of the God

Name	Tree	Horns	Animal	Serpent	Underworld Guide	Rebirth	Dismembered	Shape Shifter	Trickster	Judge	Fertility	Associated Goddess	Wisdom	Object
Adonis	Myrrh		Boar			Yes	Gored				Yes	Aphrodite		
Attis	Pine		Boar			Yes	Castrated				Yes	Cybele		Sickle
Dumuzi	Date		Herdsman			Yes	Beaten				Yes	Inanna		
Tammuz	Pine		Herdsman			Yes	Beaten				Yes	Ishtar		
Freyr	Pine	Yes	Boar/stag		Yes	Yes	Gored				Yes	Freya		Sword
Baal	Cedar	Yes	Bull/boar	Yes		Yes	Yes				Yes	Anat		Spear
Cernunnos	Yes	Yes	Lord/stag	Yes		Yes		Yes			Yes		Yes	Torc
Shiva	Peepal	Yes	Lord/bull	Cobra		Yes	Decapitated	Yes			Yes	Kali	Yes	Trident
Dionysos	Ivy	Yes	Bull	Yes		Yes	Yes	Yes	Yes		Yes	Ariadne		
Math	Yes	Yes	Bear			Yes		Yes	Yes	Yes	Yes		Yes	Staff
Osiris	Erica	Yes	Bull			Yes	Yes			Yes	Yes	Isis	Yes	Column
Tezcatlipoca	Copal		Jaguar	Yes		Yes	Sacrifice	Yes	Yes	Yes			Yes	Mirror
Bran	Alder		Raven			Yes	Decapitated	Yes					Yes	Cauldron
Odin	Ash/Yew		Raven/wolf	Yes	Yes		Hanged	Yes				Frigg	Yes	Spear
Gwynn ap Nudd		Yes	Horse	Yes	Yes	Yes					Yes	Creiddylad	Yes	
Wild Herdsman	Yes	Yes	Lord/stag	Yes	Yes	Yes	Decapitated	Yes	Yes		Yes		Yes	Club
Green Man	Yes	Yes				Yes	Decapitated	Yes	Yes		Yes		Yes	
Wild Man	Yes	Yes	Wolf?	Yes	Yes			Yes	Yes		Yes			
Robin Hood	Yes	Yes	Stag/robin			Yes	Shot	Yes	Yes		Yes	Mari-Anna	Yes	Bow
Pan	Yes	Yes	Lord/goat	Yes				Yes	Yes		Yes	Selene		Crook

Name	Tree	Horns	Animal	Serpent	Underworld Guide	Rebirth	Dismembered	Shape Shifter	Trickster	Judge	Fertility	Associated Goddess	Wisdom	Object
Anubis		Yes	Jackal		Yes	Yes	Yes			Yes				
Mara/Yama		Yes	Eleph/Bull		Yes		Yes	Yes		Yes				Chopper
Thoth		Yes	Ibis		Yes					Yes			Yes	Stylus?
Hades			Dog		Yes					Yes	Yes	Persephone		
Hermes		Yes	Ram	Yes	Yes			Yes		Yes	Yes		Yes	Staff
Manannan			Horse/boar		Yes			Yes			Yes	Rhiannon	Yes	Crane Bag
Set		Yes	Boar	Yes				Yes				Nephythys		
Loki		Yes	Fly	Yes				Yes						Sword
Lucifer	Yes	Yes	Goat?	Yes				Yes			Yes		Yes	Trident
Lugh	Ash		Horse/raven		Yes			Yes					Yes	Sword

The aspects selected are not exhaustive, although some are indispensable. Some aspects are tenuous, some are essential. While the identification of many of the deities with a tree for example is complete, in the case of Lucifer the tree is only there as it figures strongly in his myth. Some deities are associated with more than one animal. In cases where they are not a Lord of the Animals, only the main one or two animals are noted. The same is true of the associated Goddess or object. The divisions of the table are approximately one of Classical Dying and Rising Gods, Gods who share most of the defining features of the Underworld God, Nature Gods, and other deities whose function is more specialised. They are the guide to the Underworld, a trickster, a judge and so on. The table is not meant to make any statement. It is only here for those who like such things.

of the divine and tools are quite easy to find. Humans as tool makers, shaping the world around them, using the gift of hand-eye-brain, have provided the greatest leaps in awareness that life on earth has ever seen.

The evidence shows that early in time, the God of Craft was perceived as having the skill and knowledge to mould the elements of the earth. The fire, water, wood, the minerals, and the stones of the earth, responded to his touch. He had the ability to crush bones, flake stones, meld with sinew and resin, hunt, harvest and preserve. His aspect as a craftsman was easily integrated with that of magician, alchemist, shaman and shapeshifter. He has the ability to enter the dark, hot, potentially dangerous places and mine the riches that lie there. He knows how to refine materials through fire, pressure, and precise combination of elements. He knows how to produce the goods people need, allowing them greater comfort, greater beauty, greater ability, and greater power to either harm or help each other.

With this skill came authority and responsibility. With the technology of the Agricultural Revolution, men, through the divine symbolism of the God as craftsman, became aware of the suffering as well as the benefits caused by technology. Much energy was put into the propitiation of the spirits of the earth through the development of megalithic and temple building technology. The God of Craft knows his skill is but one of the many that create a healthy society. He teaches how to use the study and science of material things for the benefit and the peace of all. Thoth, the ancient Egyptian God of Craft and Science, was also an ethicist and the God of Wisdom. The weapons of the Welsh Smith God Govannon were deadly but could also heal. The temple engineer and the Smith God had their place beside the poet and the bard in preserving the order of society.

Over time, the evidence shows that the role of the God of Craft became stripped of its authority and responsibility. In the Greek pantheon, the smith god Hephaistos became a lame, bumbling fool, ridiculed for his love of Aphrodite and Athene, and indeed for his love of women in general. This shows that the all-important partnership between the craftsman God and the Goddess was broken. In popular fiction, the Roman Smith God Vulcan is no longer a God, but a planet that is home for beings devoid of emotion and ruled by logic. Diancecht, the healer of the Tuatha De Danann and maker of the silver hand for their king, Nuadha, is said to have lost his mind and destroyed the knowledge of his craft. More recently, Newton and other mathematicians were despised by visionaries such as William Blake who saw them as the anti-God. Divorced from life as a whole, separated from the realm of the Goddess and women, and made inferior to those who govern, the God of Craft, science, technology and, indeed all work in general, has become a force adrift, without ethical moorings, driven by the demand to profit and produce. He may serve the world, but he may also destroy it.

For science and technology to no longer contribute to the cause of environmental destruction but in fact become part of the essential work of restoring the environment of the earth in the 21st century, it is necessary to restore the symbolic aspects of the God as craftsman to the whole image of the divine masculine. This aspect of the God above all others needs to find his lover. Science is sexy. The intellect is cool. The technician is a sensuous explorer of life's secrets. Physics surfs the wave of the universe's beauty, and mathematics is not the realm of the Newtonian anti-God. They are imbued with the sacred images of our deepest, most profound desires.

Goibniu – The Irish Smith God, builder and architect, known in Wales as Govannon, and in England as Wayland. His brother is Amaethon, God of Agriculture. Goibniu presides over the Otherworldly Feast. From his thunderous forge come weapons for the Warrior Gods. They never miss their target and are always fatal. ANo spear made by my hand," says Goibnui, "will miss its mark, and no man who it touches will taste life again." Yet the Smith God can also heal, and those who drink his ale at the Otherworldly Feast, become immortal. In the Welsh Druid tradition the Chief Smith was reckoned the equal of the Chief Bard. His marriage to his equivalent among the women was considered crucial.

Thoth – The Egyptian Ibis-headed God of Magic, Divination and Wisdom. Thoth is often shown accompanied by a baboon and by

Anubis, the Jackal God. His domain includes music, medicine, geometry, architecture, astronomy, drawing and writing – hieroglyphics. Thoth is the measurer of time, the Divine Judge and the Moon God. He wears the lunar crescent and disc. One of the most ancient of gods, Thoth is the bearer of the magic formula that enables the dead to pass through the trials of the Underworld.

The Greeks identified Thoth with Hermes, the messenger between the worlds. They called him Hermes Trismegistos 'Thrice Great Hermes.' His tradition became developed in Greek Alexandria and formed the basis for Western Hermeticism. This is a rich esoteric teaching that rejects ontological dualism and emphasises the positive aspects of the universe.

14

God of Magic

The magician is a creator who uses knowledge of how the natural world and the universe work to cause an effect. He works with the miraculous laws of life to effect transformation. The imagery of the God offers men the potential for the greatest transformation they will ever be asked to make.

The ancient mythic God by definition has magical abilities attributed to him. Thoth, the divine craftsman, and Manannan, God of the Sea and the Otherworld, are magicians. Robin Hood has his hedgerow magic. The God shape shifts and morphs into every form. Yet there are misconceptions around magic that make it difficult to define what it is. If we put aside the tricks and illusions of the conjuror, then magic today is defined as the ability to use the will to make things happen that according to the normal laws governing matter, space and time, could not happen. If we remove the phrase "according to the normal laws governing matter, space and time" then magic is simply the art of getting what you want. OK. But put the phrase back, and magic is the manipulation of the space-matter-time continuum in a manner that is unnatural to it.

This, as perhaps we always suspected, gives the game away: magic is unnatural. Yet, also as we suspect, no one has ever cheated on the laws of nature, for the simple reason it cannot or has not yet been done. This is not being cynical. The proof of it is shown in reflecting on the fact that one abnormality in the laws of space-matter-time in the universe as we know it, would set in motion a chain of events that could not exist simultaneously within the present chain of events. It would create an alternative universe where the magical act – the abnormality – would in fact, be normal. It would create a universe where the laws of physics are different to those that currently prevail in this one. Unless a way is found to hop from one universe to another, magic as it is currently defined, that is as "unnatural," is impossible.

If magic was to be redefined however to mean the way things happen according to the natural laws that govern matter, space and time, then, contrary to the prevailing notion that the realm of the God and Goddess is unnatural, then we would already be in the realm of the God and the Goddess. In this realm, and under this definition, the magician is a creator who uses knowledge of how the natural world and the universe work to cause an effect. The God in his aspect of Thoth and Manannan demonstrates this ability. They work with the miraculous laws of life to effect transformation, and that is an excellent definition of magic. As lunar gods, their method is shown in the phases of the moon: waning, dark, waxing and full. They know when to give way, when to die, when to press ahead, and when to succeed. They tap the deep sources of creativity in life, so what they do unfolds abundantly according to natural law.

The challenge facing men today in a world of technology that allows almost anything to happen, is to integrate the symbols of the Craftsman God with those of the God as Magician. Technology is magic. Magic is technology. It is as much a challenge for those who want their gods to be mysterious, magical and beyond definition, to allow in the laws of the natural world, as it is for those whose gods are quantifiable, logical and mechanical, to allow in the power of the mythic image. In truth there is no contradiction. It is only the suspicions of each that continue to drive them apart.

Bran – A Celtic giant, bard and King of the Underworld. A son of Llyr, the 'sea.' In the struggle between the Children of Llyr and the Children of Don, the 'sky,' Gwydion wins three boons for humanity – the dog, the deer and the lapwing, by defeating Bran. In the war against Ireland, Bran carries his musicians on his shoulders through the sea, and then makes a bridge for his forces with his huge body. But Bran is mortally wounded in the foot by a spear. He commands the seven who escape with him to decapitate him and set his head upon White Hill where the Tower of London now stands. For eighty-seven years the Wondrous Head of Bran the Blessed entertains the assembly with its wisdom and songs. When finally placed on White Hill the divine head ensures no harm will befall the land. Bran possesses a magical vessel, which has the power of restoring the life of any placed within it. It will not restore their speech. Bran becomes Bron in the Arthurian Legends, the bringer of the Holy Grail to Britain. His tree is the alder, his bird is the raven.

Nuadha – Nuadha Argetlamh, 'of the Silver Hand,' is a king of the Tuatha de Danaan. They now live as the magical Fairy race in the hills and mounds of Ireland. Nuadha is possibly, or was for a short time, the husband of the supernatural Great Triple Goddess, the Morrigan or Morrigu, 'Great Queen' and Battle Goddess. Nuadha's miraculous hand was made by Diancecht, the great healer and craftsman of the Tuatha de Danaan.

15

The Dual Character of the God

The God carries all ambiguities within himself. He cannot be confined or defined. He is dark and light, good and evil, known and unknown. He contains all the shades and contingencies that colour existence. He moves when it is possible to move, and keeps still when it is possible to keep still.

Apart from the dualistic distinction between the Light God and the Dark God, the Gods of Heaven and those of the Underworld, a duality or an ambiguity still appears in the nature of the God. He is after all, a dying and rising God. He is always coming or going. Osiris and Set for example, form a doublet. Set appears as the destroyer and Osiris as the life giver, but both appear in a manner that suggests they are aspects of the same god. Odin and Loki may also be seen as a pair. Both gods draw their power from the Underworld realms, but Odin's wisdom and seriousness is complemented by Loki's cunning and mischievousness. The God Hermes or Mercury is fundamentally multifarious in his nature. Like the mind, he is slippery and ambivalent. He is both the patron of travellers and of the thieves who would rob them. Hermes son, Hermaphrodite, unites both sexes within himself.

The Meso-American Tezcatlipoca and Queztalcoatl are another example of this duality. Both are Lords of the Underworld, but Tezcatlipoca manifests the corrupt and violent aspects of death, while Queztalcoatl manifests the fertile and prosperous aspects. The fact there are four Tezcatlipocas may mean the Nahuatl make even more shades of distinction between the aspects of the God. When the two gods realise their struggle has no end, they unite and rest the sky on two mighty trees. Sometimes Queztalcoatl himself is represented as a doublet. He has one face of life, one face of death.

A similar image of the two-faced god appears in early European sculpture. Janus is the Roman God of doorways, both entrance and exit. Many Celtic shrines feature a similar two-faced male deity, although we know little about who he was. The Classical Underworld Gods, Hades and Pluto, are also represented as a doublet. Could their example throw illumination on the little known Celtic Horned Gods, Esus and Cernunnos? Esus, like Pluto, is the outer manifestation of the fertile and life-giving aspects of the Dark God. Cernunnos, like Hades, represents the deeper, more deadly, perhaps vision-questing aspects. Such a duality also underlies the idea of the Gods who annually alternate between the Underworld and this world. Baal, Osiris, Marduk and Adonis, all enter the Underworld and are confronted by a terrible serpent, which is an aspect of themselves. They die as an animal, the seed, the harvested fruit, vegetable and grain, and are reconstituted as food and drink for the life of the people.

Eventually this inherent ambivalence, or aspectual character, set in motion an illogicality that resulted in a schism in the God. Marduk destroys the she-monster Tiamat and creates the world out of her body. The Goddess, and the aspect of her son Marduk who journeyed into death, are denied. Thus fragmented, Marduk becomes an all-powerful creator and Sky God. The Sky Gods establish their domains 'forever,' after the prehistoric migrations of the Indo-Europeans. The chthonic local Gods of the European Neolithic and Bronze Ages were considered inferior, dark and evil, and they were set upon by the warrior aspect of the incoming Sky God, the God of Thunder. Eventually these deities were in turn portrayed as evil by other peoples, who sought in their monotheistic religion legitimation of their own state and its patriarchal system of power. Assuming the adage, "The gods of one culture become the demons of the next," we may imagine a Sky God, such as Baal, setting upon the deities before him, and in turn being set upon, and dispossessed by Yahweh.

Whatever the case, it is likely that the dualities, doublets, and alternating nature of the God represent an attempt to think about the all-inclusive character of the mythic image of the divine masculine in the face of his apparent paradox. The divine images, like the self, contain within themselves both good and evil. Only the logical-rational mind desires to separate out the natural ambivalence of good and evil into distinct polarities and define it in doctrine.

Some of the Gods do manage to remain more inclusive over the course of history than others. The Near-Eastern deity Astraios for example, is a God of the Night, but it can also be argued he is a Sky God, ruling over the Stars. The Gods: Odin, Tezcatlipoca, Shiva, Cernunnos, Dionysos and Shiva, are destroyers and death-bringers, but they are also phallic fertility-givers, musician-dancers, and the Lord of the Animals. Odin gives a mystical, wise form to the otherwise lustful, besotted, and drunken energies of the hunter and warrior. Dionysos adds madness, intoxication, frenzy – all that which is the antithesis of the order of culture – to the otherwise liberating rites of spring. Through the mirror of the ambivalent God, participants in their rites can find a means of knowing and thus integrating all that which is 'other,' alien or fear-filled.

Apep – The serpent or crocodile form of Set. Every night Apep attempts to swallow the sun to prevent it rising in the east. Every morning he is defeated, but restores himself to fight again. During an eclipse Apep has greater power to destroy the order of the world.

Baphomet – A hermaphroditic personification of the God and Goddess used in the initiation rites of the Knights Templar. Baphomet has a goat's head, horns and legs, a woman's breasts and a man's arms. On the head is the Pythagorean pentacle, the Greek *baphemetous*. Above it is a pillar of flame. Inscribed on one arm is *coagula* and on the other *solve* – the coagulating and dissolving principles of alchemy. Rising from the genitals is a caduceus with twin serpents, surmounted by a rainbow. Baphomet represents the joining of all polarities and all natures. Like Hermes, Baphomet is both good and evil, human and animal, male and female, God and Goddess. The use of Baphomet in ritual led to the persecution of the Templars by the Inquisition.

Mordred – In British mythology and in the Grail mysteries Mordred is the son, nephew, and perpetual rival of King Arthur. He is born either of Morgan or, more likely, of Morgause, the 'Mother,' Queen of the North, the middle of Arthur's three sisters. They are in the line of the sovereign monarchs of Britain, who include Bran the Blessed. Mordred is the Dark Prince whose enmity, along with that of his mother, is said to be responsible for the downfall of Arthur and the Round Table.

Mordred fatally wounds Arthur in battle, before being struck down himself. Beneath the well-known story lies a wealth of hidden meaning. Morgan, Morgause and their third sister, Elaine or Anna, are the Great Triple Goddess. Arthur, the 'Bear,' is the zoomorphic, Rising and Falling God. He dies but will return. Like Osiris and Cronos he has children through the line of his sister, the Great Mother Goddess. The Arthurian legends contain the ancient traditions of the God, but they are obscured beneath layers of transcendent monotheism. The Triple Goddess is concealed under the stigma of darkness. Mordred, the Lord of the Waning Year and all that he represents, has become evil. Only his 'good' brother, Gawain, a Lord of the Waxing Year, is honoured.

Mordred, Melwas or Medrawt – abductor of Guinevere, the Flower Bride and Solar Goddess – reveals the dual aspect of the God. He is one of the eternal combatants by whom the waxing and waning order of the worlds, and the male-female polarity, is maintained.

16

Darkness and Light — The Lunar God

And somewhere deeper still there is a terrible scene — a tearing, a dismembering, a devouring. It is hard to see. Did we really do that? This corner of the Underworld insists we did. Somewhere far down in phyletic memory it dawns upon us that we too participated in the original communion feast. Yes. While the drumbeat pounded in our heads, we too plumbed that depth. Such things became our primary taboos, and at the same time, the most ecstatic, most potent fulfilment of our desires.

While the Western world has developed many mystical and scientific doctrines of light it entirely lacks a comparative doctrine of darkness. Although it may be argued that darkness is simply the absence of light, the presence of darkness in the universe is a significant and unquestionable fact. We spend half our lives in the night and the view into space is made outstanding by the infinite expanse of utter darkness. Indeed much of the matter of the universe has become mysteriously veiled from our eyes, from our mechanical sensors and from our mathematics by darkness. This would not be disconcerting were it not for the fact that in the binary opposition of light and dark we prefer the light. Light is evaluated as good, desirable, positive, supreme, ideal, ultimate, and all-powerful.

As it stands, the ethical evaluation placed upon light amounts to a discrimination against darkness! Neo-Platonist, Gnostic, and many Christian sects regard light as being of the spirit and darkness as being the opposite, that is, of evil and the world. At its most extreme it is said that achievement of spiritual heights is synonymous with the self being 'turned to light.' In cases where the dark is acknowledged as having some value, it nevertheless is viewed as merely being a stage to pass through before returning to the ideal state of the light. Darkness in and of itself is treated as an adjunct, maybe a necessary one, but still an adjunct to the light. The journey to the Underworld is important only for the journey through the Underworld, and it merely precedes the return to the light. In the natural world, we find the dark of the moon not acknowledged, but referred to it in terms of what comes after it, that is, it is called the new moon.

Originally it appears that prehistorical spirituality did not place such an ethical evaluation upon white and black, light and darkness. Blackness was the colour of the fertile earth and thus of life and health. White was the colour of bones, of anemia and death. The return of the waxing moon was preceded by the acknowledgement of the three dark nights of no moon. The emphasis was upon the whole cycle. Even the rural pagans of the Classical world knew that only by going into the dark could the riches contained there be found. Without creating a dualism, paganism treated light and dark, summer and winter, life and death, as two halves of a cyclical whole. Gradually however, the mythic idea of the God undergoing the journey around the cycle of life and death, mostly as a god of seasonal vegetation, meant he began to be perceived as two-fold. He had a waxing and a waning aspect. Eventually the god in the heavens was no longer perceived as being the same as the god in the underworld; each died to and was replaced by the other. The Bronze and Iron Age Dying and Rising Gods were still contained within the cycle of the whole as they alternated between the worlds, but the nature of the archetypal masculine meant that their heavenly and underworld aspects became quite distinct. The Goddess did not become two-fold. Her life-creating and life-taking aspects – the dark womb and the dark tomb – always remained contained within her archetypal form. The Goddess is always all things simultaneously. It is the God who divides.

A truly dualistic position was achieved with the claim that two metaphysically irreducible forces created the universe. This was a logical development of the mythic idea of the twin gods.

71

This worldview appears in Eurasia as early as the 3rd millennium B.C.E. with the advent of the Sky God worshipping Indo-Europeans. The God of Thunder – such as the later Yahweh, Zeus and Thor – wrestles with the forces of darkness. In the case of Persian Zoastrianism this was the perennial struggle between the forces of good and the forces of evil. Here, Ahura Mazda is the good god who struggles with his brother Ahriman, the god of evil, on the battleground of earth. Needless to say, Ahura Mazda is the God of Light and Ahriman the God of Darkness.

In creating a doctrine of mystical darkness it is not necessary to go to the extreme of dualism. Opposites such as light and dark, male and female, high and low, good and evil, are not dualistic unless treated that way in a metaphysical doctrine or cosmology. Opposites simply indicate that a polarity of principles exist in creation and in the mind. Life provides many examples of polarities and paradoxes without demanding a dualistic doctrine to explain them. The waxing and waning phases of the moon for example, does not mean there are two moons.

The Celtic imagery of the God was contained by all the phases of the moon – a memory of which is handed down in 'the man in the moon.' The God Hermes, or Thoth, rules the mind, and his nature by definition is ambivalent, quick, androgynous and paradoxical. His character suggests no need of a rational explanation for everything. In psychology every archetype is considered to contain its own opposite. The archetypes have a polarised character – each mythological deity, such as Hermes, is both good and bad. The image of the cosmos as a cycle, containing every polarity, can comfortably integrate a mystical idea of darkness. Yet it remains that many mystical doctrines of light exist, while its polar opposite the dark, is tarred by the brush of discrimination.

The progress of the elevation of the light historically coincides with the rise of patriarchy. The most powerful patriarchal gods are identified with the sun. They triumph over the cyclical lunar image of the God and the cosmos. Their epithets insist that they rise eternally – they 'live forever.' They do not change or die, thus they cannot be reborn. Zeus, Yahweh and Apollo are good examples of this god. Patriarchal solar symbols are to be found in a distribution pattern that suggests they arrived in Europe from the east over the late 3rd to the 1st millennium B.C.E. The solar gods became the guardians of the rational laws patriarchy required to maintain its systems of hierarchical authority, militancy, primogeniture, inheritance and ownership. The God of Light, of the Sky, of the Sun, was, and still is, associated with authority and kingship. As guardians of the law, the Light Gods were elevated to being gods of justice, and from there it was an easy step to their becoming gods of good. Sun and thus light is good, darkness is bad. Heaven now becomes a place of eternal light, inhabited by the Creator Father God. Hell is conceived as a dark, gloomy, irredeemable place of shadow. Rebirth no longer has a place in the cosmology, and duality was in the making.

The pantheistic Greeks and Romans however always treated their deities as being divinely immanent, wherever they were, and the Underworld deities still thrived among the rural classes in the classical world. The names of their Underworld deities, Pluto and Dispater, literally mean 'wealth.' In Egypt the struggle between light and dark, good and evil, life and death, was personified in Osiris and Set – and subsequently in the struggle between the son of Osiris, Horus, and Set. It was said that in the "Sphere of the Eternal" all such dualities cease. It was taught in the script known as *The Secret of the Two Partners* that all dualities are one, and this oneness was present in the Pharaoh. The Pharaoh was thus both Osiris and Set, light and dark, male and female.

Non-scriptural Judaistic and then Christian thought identified darkness with Satan and light with God. The Church Fathers such as Augustine and Thomas Aquinas used the metaphor of darkness and light freely. Luther, Dante and Milton continued this usage. It is ironic that the last two chose Lucifer 'Light Bringer,' to be the name of their dark king of hell. Lucifer may once have been the God of Light for a patriarchal race with much in common with Christianity. But Lucifer may be better interpreted as the being who reveals or has the courage to go into that which otherwise would remain hidden.

What does this mean? Who dares go into the dark? In medieval alchemy the stage of blackness – the *nigredo* – in the process of spiritual transmutation, was precisely that of going into the unknown darkness and releasing the potential contained there. In magic, what is rarely understood is that those who walk the 'left-hand' path are deliberately working with energy of the dark half of the day, the dark half of the year, the dark phase of the lunar cycle. In current esoteric traditions such as the Kabbalah and Western Hermeticism, every effort is being made to restore the Dark to the vital role it plays in the cyclical, regenerative view of the cosmos. This is beginning to move toward a mystical doctrine of darkness.

Every journey into the darkness contains a graphic description of the topography of the Underworld, compared to which the descriptions of heaven are sadly lacking. The Celtic legends describe Blessed Isles, often 'below the waves,' where none lack for sport and nourishment. The Mayan Underworld is a paradisiacal realm of fragrant flowers and luxuriant forests. The Buddhist Otherworlds describe a variety of Heaven, intermediate, Hell, and Buddhic realms. The Egyptian land of Tuat has precise regions, ordeals and trials. The iconography and the form of the megalithic monuments suggest the Neolithic European idea of the Underworld as a dark womb of cyclical regeneration. The Palaeolithic realm of the cave with its animals and masked dancers in the deepest recesses, suggests a distinct character and role for the Underworld. The descriptions of the Underworld in Classical mythology are extremely detailed. Several significant features stand out. Let us enter.

There is a river, the Styx, fed by four tributaries. A coin given to the surly Ferryman Charon, secures the crossing. A fierce dog guards the entranceway. The dog is black, or red and white. It may be many-headed or a pack. Unlike Heracles, who crushed the dog and dragged it back to the human world, we are courteous and offer it what we have. Various regions lie on either side. There may be three, there may be six, there may be twelve. Some are considered more advantageous than others. Various springs flow through these regions. Some are poisonous, some thirst quenching, some delicious, some bring memory, others forgetfulness and oblivion. The trees of the Underworld are Black and White Poplar, Cypress, Yew, Pomegranate and

Apple. The apple seems particularly delightful to those in the paradise realms. Looking about, there are locations where individuals
suffer a particular torment. Prometheus is chained to a rock and
his perpetually renewing liver is torn out daily by an eagle.
Other Giants groan under slabs of rock or in remote depths.
The Giants were banished here by the Gods. The suggestion is
that their true place is elsewhere, perhaps in the world above as
benefactors, like Prometheus, of humanity.

There are animals here too. On the one hand, they may be here
because they are considered to have no soul. They may be here
because they have a soul but prefer to remain discarnate in the
Underworld than suffer the terrible torments in the world above.
They may be here as they no longer have a place in the world
above. Whatever the case, the crimes against them are surely terrible.
It is possible that some of the shrieking we hear in the distance comes
from those who judge themselves as the tormentors of animals. On
the other hand, the animals may be here to remind us of their eternal
presence alongside our presence on earth. The animal spirit form
that moves the many particular forms in the world above joins us
for a while. Their forms are outlined in ochre on shadowy walls.
It is tempting to put on animal masks and dance the deer, the
buffalo, the wild auroch, the eagle. But not this time. We move on.

There are places that seem particularly noxious, locked up, hard to
get a glimpse at. We may identify a moment of incredible anxiety or
guilt. A neglected parent. An abused child. Beaten, imprisoned,
tortured faces. And what is this? A wild figure appears with an enormous erection. Music throbs in our ears. He pursues nymphs who flee
and Maenads who do not. Satyrs and other Gods arrive and join in
the general melee. Eros flies above. Suddenly there is a hush. The
crowd parts, and a beautiful mature woman is exposed sitting upon
a stone. Who will be her lover? She is sister and mother to them
all. A lovely but effeminate young man walks by. His eyes and the
woman's eyes are locked together. Someone whispers, "They have
been lovers since the womb." The boy mounts the stone. The dark
vault of forbidden love looms. But not for us. We turn away.

And somewhere deeper still, a terrible moment of absolute abandonment – a tearing, a dismembering, a devouring. Blood flies

everywhere. It is hard to see. Did we really do that? This corner of the Underworld insists we did. Somewhere far down in phyletic memory it dawns upon us that we too participated in the original communion feast. Yes. While the drumbeat pounded in our heads, we too plumbed that depth. And it lead to further orgies of sex and violence. Such things became our primary taboos, and at the same time, they became the most ecstatic, most potent fulfilment of our desires. We shiver at the images. Can this be all? There must be more in this place than sex, or love, or jealousy, or hunger, or incest, or fratricide, or death, or loss of self ...

As we walk on, surveying the territory, we eventually arrive at an abyss. It is the deep of Tartarus, the abode of Night, encircled by Erebus, son of Chaos. Some say it was the whirl of Chaos uniting with Tartarus that gave birth to the Earth Goddess, Gaia. Some say that the God of All Things emerged from the membrane of Chaos and divided and ordered all into creation. Others say Eros was always there from the beginning as a primordial principle, inspiring the creation to come about. Yet others say it was the Goddess of All Things who arose from Chaos and of herself gave birth to the creation. Some say only Dionysos can go here. But behind them all is not light, but utter Darkness. On this all are agreed. Nothing stirs in the depths. The drums become silent. If we dare go deeper, even the surrounding dance of Chaos falls away. What remains is complete and utter Darkness.

Cronos – After Uranus, the Sky, fathered the Titans upon Gaia, the Earth, he thrust the Cyclopes back into Tartarus. Gaia swore revenge for the loss of her children and persuaded the Titans to attack Uranus. The Titans, led by Cronos, were successful. Cronos castrated his father with a flint sickle. The drops of blood formed the Three Fates, Aphrodite, and the Giants. Cronos then began a long rule on earth described as both a Golden Age and a tyranny. Fearing usurpation, Cronos swallowed the children which Rhea, the daughter of Gaia, bore him.

Cronos rules over the Underworld realm of Elysium, adjacent to Hades' domains. It is a paradise realm, similar to Avalon, full of music, whose inhabitants may be reborn whenever they please.

The name of Cronos may mean 'time' but is more likely to derive from crow. The crow is a bird of divination associated with the Roman Saturn and the British Kings Bran and Arthur. Both kings rule over a Golden Age. Their protection and aid can be evoked in the present and in time of future need. Saturn is the Roman Cronos, from whose curved pruning hook we get the image of old Father Time. Cronos or Saturn as Lord of Death has the power to bring about cycles of destruction that are nonetheless capable of restoring the primal Golden Age. He thus presides over the Saturnalia, the return to natural law.

Erebus – A primeval Greek God of the Underworld. Son of Chaos, brother and wife to Nyx, father of Nemesis, Eros and Charon. Erebus is the personification of the circles of lesser darkness proceeding outward from the black depths of Tartarus.

Dionysos – The Greek God of Wine, born of the Moon, whose androgynous and terrible aspects are the typification and revelation of 'otherness.' He leads his celebrants, including a host of Satyrs and Maenads, but mostly women, into frenzy, rapture, mania and murder. They strip away all convention and their wild animal nature is exposed. They devour raw meat. They become everything a citizen of the ordered state is not allowed to be. They reveal the bloodthirstiness of the womb, of birth giving.

Only Dionysos is said to be able to plumb the depths of Tartarus. As a child Dionysos had horns and bore a crown of serpents. His plants include the ivy, pine, vine and pomegranate. His popularity accompanied the Cult of the Vine and Orphic thought around the Mediterranean. Dionysos is associated with trees in general and is probably descended from an ancient Neolithic god of the annual cycle of vegetation. The members of his cult await his return during winter, celebrate his epiphany and gradual increase during spring, and then participate in the orgy of madness that accompanies the dismemberment and eating of the God.

Dionysos is the Lord of Dementia and ecstasy – the ability to get outside of oneself. He manifests the ambivalence of all human thought about the Divine. He contains all the opposites: frenzy and purity, rapture and terror, male and female, conception and death, good and evil, order and chaos, culture and nature. He is bisexual, a dual god, both purifying and intoxicating. At several points in his long history Dionysos becomes theriomorphic, that is animal in shape. The Greek legends tell of him being a ram, a serpent, a lion, and a panther, but he is better known for being a bull. Dionysos married Ariadne, daughter of King Minos and Queen Pasiphae of Crete. They are the keepers of the Minotaur and of the labyrinthine entrance into the Underworld. Although said to be the son of Zeus and the mortal Queen Semele, the origins of Dionysos are likely to reach far back into the Palaeolithic.

Tartarus – A primeval Dark Principle or God present from the beginning and at the creation of the world. From the union of Tartarus and the Earth Mother Gaia sprang the first beings, the *Ge-antes*, the 'dwellers of the earth-before,' the Giants. Although in fact, dark, hidden and formless, the poets made Tartarus into Hell, the Realm of the Underworld. Heroes like Heracles, Theseus, Orpheus, Marduk and Bel harrow it when they visit. They struggle with the Hounds of Hell, decapitate demons, crush serpents and so on and either return empty-handed or with some precious gift. To be fair, Orpheus did none of these things. He sought to be reunited with his lover.

17

The Rising, Climaxing and Falling God

The God is the serpent. He lives under earth and stone. He is red, vibrant, dangerously exotic. He is gorgeously phallic, lustfully libidinous, erotic, hard-edged, well defined, gleaming, rising and falling with sensuous lustre on his skin. He is the dancer, the flute player, weaving rhythms on the growing edge of life. He writhes in the depths of cellular exchange. He is the ecstasy of sacred power trembling in flesh and veins. He is Shiva, Set, Typhon, Adanc, Kokopelli and Pan.

It is a fact that everything which is born, dies. It follows that if everything born – or conceived – is a result of sex, then the outcome of sex is always death. In fact, biologists point to the selection of sex as the means of reproduction as necessarily including a 'death gene.' So life includes a gene for death.

The parthenogenetic system (the single or sexless dividing gene,) as a means of reproduction may not include the death gene but neither does it include the kind of diversity, intelligence and rate of adaptation we associate with sex and death. As a symbol, the threshold of the human womb, the vulva of a woman – the sexual Goddess – is beautiful and terrible. It points in both directions. It points toward childhood, birth, gestation, conception and sex – and before that, to a previous existence? It also points to the inexorable process onward from sex, the point of conception, through life, to old age and death – and beyond that, to the next existence?

Ignoring the last questions as we simply do not know the answers, and taking the human body as the model (and as we see identical processes being enacted in animals and in much of the plant world we can feel that at least here we are on firm ground,) if the womb symbolically points to sex, life and death, then what does the phallus imply? If we can arrive at the commonly held idea of the three-fold feminine: the Great Triple Goddess – Maiden, Mother, Crone, corresponding to sex, life and death – then what is the equivalent symbolic concept for the masculine? Let us describe the sexual act of reproduction.

The woman opens her thighs. The lips of the vulva open and close around the penis. The vagina holds the penis. Eggs are periodically released from the ovaries to await fertilisation in the womb. If fertilised the egg grows into a new life in the womb. After nine months the child emerges through the lips of the vulva. The man has a stiffening of the penis. In this condition the vulva and vagina can receive it. Sperm are released. The penis becomes flaccid. The phallus rises, releases and falls. It may not always release, but the womb may not always conceive. The penis may not always rise, but from this description we have the basic idea. What can be drawn from this?

In relation to the life-creating and life-taking potential of the three-fold Great Goddess, the God rises and falls. He is the child, the lover and the recipient of death in the womb of the Goddess. He is the living and the dying aspect of the whole cycle. He rises up as a child. He rises up as an impetuous lover. He releases as a mature man. He declines as a lover. He declines as a man. Sometimes he becomes wise. He dies and re-enters her womb as tomb. We have the Youth, the Man, the Old Man. The Boy, Warrior, Sage? However we say it, it doesn't sound as poetic as the Maiden, Mother, Crone. Perhaps it is the Ascending, Culminating and Descending God – the Rising, Climaxing and Falling God... the Lunar God... and why not? We have the God who undergoes the transformations of existence, reaches a goal, a zenith, enters the darkness and promises the eternal return. It is a linear wave on a spatial map of the cosmos compared to the all-encompassing particulate *prima materia* of the Goddess.

In India, the God Shiva is represented by the Lingam, a cylindrical rounded stone. The Goddess – Parvati, Durga and Kali, or Maiden, Mother, Crone – is represented by the Yoni, a flat or concave circular stone with a rim. The Lingam is placed in the centre of the Yoni. The Lingam is identified with the still centre of the Wheel of Existence. The Wheel is turned by the dynamic energy of the feminine. In ecstatic sexual union between Shiva and the Death Goddess Kali, supreme annihilation is brought about. Shiva rises, climaxes, and, at this point, Kali is shown holding a decapitated head, or she is decapitating Shiva's head. From here on, only total transformation, rebirth, and regeneration is possible. Shiva or his bull bear the horns of the waxing and waning lunar epiphany upon their heads.

A similar theme is to be found in the ancient European traditions of the Sacred King. At the end of the reign of the King who embodies the God, the land, and the spirit of fertility, he is slain. There is record of dismemberment and even devouring of his flesh. He then enters the earth, a willing sacrifice. This ensures the end of the old cycle and the beginning of a newly potent one. Through imitation of the lunar cycle, regeneration is possible on the earth.

In some places, or everywhere after some time, a surrogate, perhaps an animal, was killed and eaten in the place of the King. Eventually the rite became one of the barley – the Grain God. He dies by being put into the ground. Then he is decapitated at the hand of the reaper. Then he may die again in grinding, in fermentation, or in the fire. All this ensures that the wealth and fertility of the realm and its people are perpetually renewed. Remnants of this tradition are common in local folklore. A scapegoat, a straw figure, an effigy, is destroyed. A ritual communion, originally orgiastic, later a more civilised feast, is participated in. Offerings are made to the earth. There is a death, and then life can rise transformed. Such traditions were widespread in Meso-America and in Africa as recently as colonisation. The universality of the tradition points toward a possible three-fold form for the God. This can be characterised as a Waxing God and a Waning God, with points of transformation either in sex or death in-between.

Apart from the lunar cycle, if we identify – as it seems our ancestors did – this three-fold God with the cycle of the year, then there is a stage of ascendance and a stage of descendance. The God rises in the form of the Spirit of the Waxing Year, and then descends in the form of the Spirit of the Waning Year. In the Neolithic European figurines these forms correspond to the ithyphallic youthful God and then the introspective, mature or aged God. This creates an annual dual rhythm for the God with two points of transformation in-between.

One point of transformation is at the beginning of summer and the other is at the beginning of winter. In the Celtic cycle of the year, the third form of the God emerges as the Lord of Sex and Fertility at Beltane in spring. The Beltane rites are gorgeously phallic, rather rude, and include ritualised marriages of a Wild King, perhaps in animal form, with a May Queen – who is, by comparison, rather urbane and civilised in her jewellery and long train. Then the God emerges again, six months later, at Samhain or Halloween in the fall. But this time he is the Lord of Death. He is the reaper and the reaped, the barley in the fermenting vats, the grain between two stones. The women mourn his loss. One figurine found in Hungary dating to the 5th millennium B.C.E. shows the God with a hook or sickle over his shoulder. The hook is common to Attis, Cronos, Mara and Yama as Lords of Death.

Spring and Autumn, rising and descending, sprouting from the earth and entering the earth, fertility and death – all these are the dominant themes of the God.

The Rites of the God don't necessarily take place in such an ordered way. The Rites of Dionysos, Osiris, Baal, Tammuz and Adonis bunch up in spring and summer. They enact all the stages described above, but over a shorter, perhaps a lunar, period. There may be a preference being demonstrated here for the God of the Waxing Year; but his climax and death always fall in short order behind. This focus may also refer to the fact that the God is waxing even as he wanes. By imitating the lunar cycle, death ensures rebirth. The God as animal or as vegetable – seed or plant – dies so new life can come. The grain 'dies' as it is sown into the earth, the green shoots are 'born' thereafter. But no one is going to be digging into the ground and watching the process closely; as symbol the events are simultaneous. The Mayans actually had Ascending and

Descending Gods. Their spirits rose and fell, often in serpent form, in rites conducted upon the stepped pyramids.

The linear movement of the God around the cycle of the year suggests several things. Firstly, the God, as the spirit of vegetation, rises in late winter and the spring. He is potent and able to enhance the increasing power of the Goddess – the Earth. His phallus enters the earth, as for example in the rites of copulation practiced in the fields of early and Medieval Europe. As in real life, the virile member of the God then falls. Sex and insemination mean darkness and death. The God put in the furrow of the Earth Goddess, dies. Death means rebirth. An understanding of this is vividly depicted in Palaeolithic cave art where the hunter and his spear are shown in the same relationship to a game animal as the erect penis is to the vulva. Both lead to a 'wounding,' which is death – the animal, the man and the penis all fall – but through provision of nourishment and birth, they give further life. The animal and the vulva proliferate through the death of the God as hunter.

Secondly, and following on from this, the two points of transition by the God on the threshold of the womb, express an ambivalence about the mother. The man – his spear, his penis – enters the 'wound' of the Great Mother, a woman or animal. His penis 'dies' and the animal dies, but nourishment is provided. The man then emerges from the womb – but now he is a helpless child. Moreover, he does not emerge from any womb, but from the womb of his mother – the giver of his life. The man simultaneously desires to enter the womb of his mother – to retrieve his virility – but fears it, as it also means helplessness, dependence, and death. He must die like the animal, be reborn like the grain. The man can only go there in total abandonment – total annihilation. A part of him dies with the animal.

The Rising and Falling God undergoes two turning points in the cycle of existence. Both of these take place before and within the regenerative womb of the Great Mother. In each case he dies and is reborn by her. This is the possible significance of the many Neolithic temples that take the form of the uterus. The shrines of Çatal Hüyük, the sanctuaries of Malta, the dolmens and passage graves of Megalithic Europe are openings into and exits from the womb of the life-creating and life-taking Earth Mother.

Thirdly, in the Iron Age, or at some point in time depending on the area, a surrogate – a scapegoat, perhaps in animal form – replaced the death of the God King. This took on the symbolic role as removing any and everything the tribe did not want. Uncontrollable aggression, violence, racial impurity, feelings of guilt, inferiority, and so on are prime examples. This externalisation of the 'other' ensured cultural and spiritual purity, and racial and gender superiority. Sacrifice put another through the process of death so the patriarchal cultural order, the priests and kings in authority, would not have to die. This is a long way from the enactment of the 'dark' emotions so that they are accepted and internalised. The tearing apart of the bodies of Dionysos and Osiris, the goring of Adonis and Diarmuid in the genitals, the castration of Attis, all seem excessive as fertility rites unless seen in this context of the internalisation of death and 'darkness.'

The devotion to the lost phallus also appears excessive unless seen as part of the dramatisation of the ritual cycle of the God. After the dismemberment of the God and, in some cases the orgiastic partaking of his flesh, the rites of the dark (in Egypt the dry) part of the year, take the form of lamenting and searching for the lost lover of the Goddess. He has fallen again. He awaits transformation in the cooking pots, the ovens and granaries of the Goddess. He is found within a tree or as growth in pots put aside for the purpose. His lost penis is remade from mud or growing shoots. Through these means, death and the 'dark' uncontrollable emotions of the wild, sexual energies are not scapegoated, but reinternalised back into the body of the culture.

Finally, and following on from this, the ecstatic and terrible rites of the God suggest a phase when the celebrants lose themselves in the unknown darkness of death. The idea of dismemberment of the God, or cutting off the penis, finds its shocking equivalent in the desire for love-making with the Mother-Sister Goddess – the return to the primal state of the womb. It is present in the thought of tearing animals limb from limb. What is the thinking present in cruel, erotic death... in necrophilia? What is the idea behind the tearing out the heart of a victim after he has spent a year as a King, copulating freely with his symbolic mother and sisters, and then putting on his flayed skin? Through abandonment of the normal limits of self, the sense of self, of 'I,' becomes expanded to include others, the tribe and even animals and nature. Through such communion all can be reborn. This is certainly suggested by the myths and rites of Osiris, Dionysos, Attis, Tezcatlipoca, Shiva, and possibly those of the Minotaur and of Pan.

Although other conclusions can be drawn from the cycle of the three-fold God around the year, a form for the God is beginning to shape up. Not the God before the Neolithic, undifferentiated from the Great Mother, nor the transcendent God of the Iron and Historical Ages, but the God who emerged from the former and from whom a partial prototype was taken for the latter. This God is Lord of the Waxing Year and Lord of the Waning Year. Then – perhaps simultaneously in his lunar hierophany – he is God of Fertility and God of Death. He is present as the wild, vivifying life energy and then he is absent. He is always rising and falling, coming and going. He is either entering the earth or rising from it. The God is the metaphor for the increase and departure of the life force of Nature – which is, in all its forms, the Goddess. The God is the active manifestation and the subject of the cycle of change. He is Youth, Man and Ancient. He undergoes birth, life, sex and death, while the Goddess is those things.

This cyclical but linear character of the male is supported by the patterns found in the traditional myths and rituals of the Neolithic and Bronze Age gods, in male sexuality, and in male behaviour in general. The male tendency is movement in a single-minded fashion toward a goal. This is fine, as long as it is remembered that this movement includes a releasing and a descending phase. The road away from the goal is as important as the road toward it. If the culture and its god-forms are always oriented to achievement, apotheosis and transcendence in a never-ending heavenly dynasty of light, then there is trouble. It is a permanent erection. There will be phallic monuments, dynasties, guns and missiles – pointing at the 'other,' the externalised darkness. There will be the denial of death, and energy technologies that can never be sustained, renewed or cleaned up. If there is a stage of letting go, a following through, a movement toward completion, death and darkness, then the cycle is complete. A new man, in harmony with the transformational character of the feminine, rises. A man who is able to meet the feminine as equal appears. Consciousness flourishes in the mythic cycle that includes every aspect of the God.

Bel – (1) A mythical ancestor and king, Beli the Great of Britain. Husband of the ancient Goddess Don and father of Arianrhod. (2) A primal thunder and lightning god, Belenus, 'shining,' whose festival of Beltane is celebrated at the beginning of May. A pan-European god of pastoralism, fire and fertility, whose rites include the driving of cattle between two fires.

(3) In ancient Babylon the God King Marduk is also known as Bel, 'lord.' He is the head of a pantheon of deities who are captured, sentenced and imprisoned in the Underworld by other gods. A round of annual rituals, including a sacred marriage with the Mother Goddess, reinstates his position. Bel-Marduk is kin to the Baals, and the Dying and Rising Gods of the Middle East whose fortunes rise and fall on an annual basis. They are co-creators with the Goddess. But by 1700 B.C.E. Marduk becomes the destroyer of the great primeval she-serpent Tiamat and the patriarchal priesthood is instated. Yahweh, without any relationship to a Goddess, is based upon this later Marduk. St Michael, the dragon killer, replaces Bel in the European tradition. The point of the earlier traditions is not to kill the dragon, but to direct its earth-arising power over the summer months into fertility. The name of another famous dragon killer, St George, means, 'earth tiller.' This elucidates the original character of Bel.

John Barleycorn – A late, rustic name for the Dying and Rising God in the British tradition. 'Sir John,' with his obvious phallic connotations, rises and falls with the fortunes of the grain. First he falls into the dark earth and dies. Then he rises again as the tender sprouts of spring and eventually the full head of grain. Then he falls to the reaper, is beaten, dismembered, and sometimes ground to death. Then he rises again in the fermentation of the bread or the beer. Then he dies again in being consumed. Finally he rises as strength in the limbs, as blood in the penis, or as inspiration in the head that sings the song which tells his story.

Minotaur – In the form that the legend comes to us, the Minotaur is not a God but a bull-headed man. He is born of a union between a white bull and the Queen of Crete, Pasiphae. He is confined in a labyrinth built by the craftsman Daedalus below the Palace of Knossos. Fed by human sacrifice, the Minotaur is slain by the Athenian hero Theseus, with the aid of the royal daughter Ariadne. Theseus promises to marry Ariadne, but abandons her on the Isle of Naxos. She is found by Dionysos and marries him.

The Minotaur legend reveals aspects of the extremely ancient mystery of the God, the Goddess and the Underworld. The labyrinth itself is a long and worthy topic of study. The most common theme among cultures with a labyrinth tradition is that it symbolises the pathway to and from the Land of the Dead. Theseus negotiates its turns, meets his primal, powerful, shadow nature, incorporates it – in a bath of blood – and so qualifies to marry Ariadne, 'most holy.' She is a Goddess, variously associated with the Spider ('arachne'), Fate, the Earth, the Moon and orgiastic rites. King Minos is a representative of the spirit of sovereignty, tied like so many ancient monarchs, to a chthonian cult of blood, the land and the sacred bull. Daedalus appears as a Thoth, an Asmodean or Math-like being, possessed of the secret formula to unravel the secrets of the Heavens and the Underworld. It is unlikely that all the mysteries contained in the legend of the Minotaur will be unravelled. But as Minoan Crete was the last surviving remnant of the matricentric Neolithic European peoples it is likely that an exploration of its archetypes will reveal much about the polymorphic pantheistic worldview.

18

Good and Evil

The inner sky of the mind fills with images, ideas and concepts on a continuous basis. Some of those ideas seem so real and so powerful they become apparently autonomous. Yet, the Gods and Goddesses are creations of our own minds. They stud the starry universe that wheels within and only within our eyes. They provide a way for consciousness to think about the whole with all its ambivalent and changing parts. They provide a functional cosmology based upon the real, observable polarity of male and female, which tells the whole story of creation. Consciousness flourishes in the mythic cycle that includes every aspect and symbol of the divine.

The story of good and evil involves a whodunit saga on the part of early Judaic and Christian theologians. Their questions include: Who committed the first sin? If God is omnipotent why does he allow evil to exist? This is called theodicy, or the problem of good and evil. To such questions, theodicy provides answers like this: If God is all good, then the wickedness and suffering that exists in the world must come from a second principle. This is the Devil. But if there is a second principle then God is not omnipotent and a dualism exists in the creation. This dualism is rejected by official Christian mono-theism in which God, by definition, is all-powerful. So the Devil must have been made by God and fell from heaven – but before the fall of humans – and God must allow the suffering he causes for a reason. Perhaps to exalt the glory of God, and to test and so establish the goodness of the faithful? But then the Devil would be working for God and not be the Devil, and God would be at least partly responsible for evil. Out of this perplexity emerges the figure of Lucifer.

One of the earliest, if not the earliest mention of Lucifer, is in Isaiah 14:12. Lucifer falls from heaven for exalting himself "above the stars of God," and for attempting to be "like the most High." For this he is "brought down to hell." Now, we happen to know that one of the main concerns of the Hebrew writers of Isaiah (and most of the Old Testament) was to dismiss and pour scorn on other gods and goddesses to help establish their own state brand of monotheism. The trend across the Near East and Eastern Europe in the last two millennia B.C.E. was for an omnipotent sky god to replace the old agricultural chthonic deities. As Yahweh rose in Israel, so did Chemos in Moab, Hadad in Damascus, Baal in Canaan, and so on. Isaiah 14 in fact originates from a Canaanite text in which a God of Light descends from heaven to earth in the form of a lightning-serpent to fertilise the Great Earth Mother. The Christian writer Origen in the third century C.E. identified Lucifer with Satan, the personification of evil, but Lucifer was originally an ancient Canaanite deity of mid-summer, the sun or the stars.

Lucifer, 'Light Bringer,' was, like Queztalcoatl, identified with Venus, the Morning Star. Both deities bear the title 'Son of the Morning.' In the ancient Near Eastern tradition – where the god possesses a cyclical regenerative character alternating between the heavens and the underworld – Lucifer is the lesser deity who takes the place of Baal, 'Lord,' in the heavens, when Baal is in the under-world. In their aspects as Lords of Light, Lucifer, and the other bright gods, come dangerously close to the Judaeo-Christian conceptualisation of God. Lucifer is too much like God. Therefore he is arrogant and must fall. The very jealousy that the later writers accuse Lucifer of is in fact their jealousy of him, the luminescent pagan deity. He is too close to heaven.

Origen – who, like the priests of Attis, castrated himself in service of his deity – puts an interesting twist on the whole matter by saying Lucifer is necessary to human existence. In the end even Lucifer will be redeemed. Without free will a valid moral choice would not exist or at least be a pointless exercise. Lucifer, the angel who made what must be considered the first act of free will by his rebellion against the divine compulsion to do good, makes the choice to sin or not, Origen wrote, entirely meaningful. Therefore Lucifer is necessary to the purposes of creation. Finally, to avoid putting the blame for evil on God because all existence proceeds from God, Origen said that evil is just an idea and the ontological reality of Satan is seriously in doubt. In fact, evil – Satan, Lucifer, Baal, whatever – is essentially and ultimately "non being." It is a merely a negation of what is positive, that is, God.

Although Church doctrine carefully avoids the dualistic position, the above shows dualistic thinking permeating Christian thought. The same is true in Islam. Satan emerges as a Christian deity, and Shaytan emerges as a Moslem deity. Satan or Shaytan has nothing to do with the complex regenerative pagan deities of earth, heaven and the underworld. Satan is the necessary counterpart to the transcendent God. The whole history of Christian and Islamic heresy is one long, and extremely bloody, account of resistance to the self-created dualism of God and Satan. Indeed, many fundamentalist interpretations of scripture view the proposal of the non-existence of a Principle of Darkness, or a 'Prince of this World,' as itself skidding dangerously close to heresy. Recent surveys show that the great majority of Westerners still believe in a real Devil – over 60% in the USA, and Shaytan is a compelling reality in the minds of many fundamentalist Moslems today.

Some of Origen's ideas were eventually declared heretical. He tried to avoid censure in his lifetime by greatly elaborating upon the tortures, punishments, hells, sins, calamities, final battles, apocalypses, and all the things one would expect to find in a decent diabology. Yet the damage was done. Origen's theodicy reveals what all the subsequent book burnings, Inquisitions, and theologians attempt to conceal. The main points are these:

Firstly, implicit within monotheism is the tendency toward dualism. If God made the creation, then it is outside of him. Nature, by implication, is subordinate to and quite separate from spirit. Nature therefore contains a force directly opposed to God. Nature is thus impure, and all attempts to undo this inference cannot be achieved within the cosmological framework of a separate creator God.

Secondly, there is an alternative polytheistic cosmology in which nature and spirit are not separate. The God happily journeys around all realms. He has many aspects and serves to symbolically represent the self. From this it may be gleaned that Lucifer has no more external reality than shall we say, a cherub? As an abstraction, as "non-being," Lucifer is simply there to constellate a vibrant, internal, archetypal realm in which free will and a cyclical, integrated view of the cosmos exists. Dangerous stuff. Next we will be arguing for the abstraction or even for the non-existence of God.

In spiritual traditions where the deity has many aspects the dualism of good and evil or the question of theodicy never arises. In ancient Egypt for example, the cosmos was perfect, spirit and nature were one, and so no theodicy was required. The attempt by Christian theologians such as Origen to answer the question of evil created a great deal of dogma that they really could have done without. A little thought about why people – not devils – do evil acts, or why God has to be defined as outside of creation, or exclusively good – or for that matter exclusively male – immediately begins to clear up the problem. A cosmos that is seen as a whole, as a unity, as a relationship, as inclusive, and connective, and a view that thinks in terms of things rather than in abstractions, are steps in the right direction. While, if it has to be given a name at all, a mystery, a life force, an ineffable primary whatsit, containing absolutely everything within or without itself, permits an agreeable solution to the question of good and evil without elevating, diminishing, separating, or genderising anything.

To be fair to monotheists, this is exactly what the great theologians, Christian, Jewish, and Moslem, have been getting at. Allah, to many, is a concept free zone. Yahweh's name cannot be spoken. Yet it is through the effort on the part of human consciousness to think and talk about these things that cosmologies come into existence. Cosmologies and all they contain: creation stories, myths, giants, gods, goddesses, angels, tricksters, are created by humans as a necessary means of ordering and making sense of the world. We owe it to ourselves to produce useful and comprehensive cosmologies if we are to think and talk about good and evil, life and death, dark and light, in an adequate manner. Monotheism was an attempt to create a useful cosmology in a particular historical context by a particular people. It is a shame its debates have become rather sterile.

To explain this more, let us begin with the proposal that the universe is infinite and in constant change. If this is accepted, then being infinite, the universe is very accommodating, and it will probably allow any and eventually every idea to be thought of, if not come into existence at some point, at some time. A cosmology or a worldview that has come into existence is there to provide a set of images or a map to help us find a way around the universe in which we live. Because the cosmology is there however, does not mean it is correct. What can happen is that the cosmology ends up creating and maintaining the reality it insists it is only trying to describe. The infinite universe obligingly accommodates itself to the bearer of the cosmology. The cosmology may even describe and conform to reality quite comprehensively for the bearer – for a while. But because the universe is in constant change, after protracted attempts to fit the whole picture into an inadequate and generally fixed picture, the universe eventually shrugs the bearer of the cosmology off, sometimes with a bang, sometimes with a sigh. The road map, the ideas, the images of deity, the language, the vocabulary, the conceptual way of thinking about things, have become sterile and no longer match up to the complex reality. This seems to be especially true when small states who are struggling to define themselves in relation to powerful neighbours, create the cosmology. It also happens when an established elite – such as a priestly or scientific clique – attempts to maintain power.

The signs that a cosmology has become rigid appear when its bearers claim its doctrines derive from God, and that they are absolute, unquestionable, infallible, divinely ordained and so on. The deities or deity, the theories or theory, lack the complexity to accommodate and make sense of the full paradoxical play of human experience. It requires a paradigm shift to move on to the next view.

Thinking in terms of sex, or male and female, provides a comprehensive view. Sex embraces a big and therefore an adequate picture. Most cultures start off with masculine and feminine as cosmos-shaping ideas in their creation stories. Even the scientific 'Big Bang' cosmological theory has a wildly sexual ring about it. A cosmology that lacks the feminine plainly cannot make sense of human experience, while cosmologies that make the feminine the source of life are in an extremely favourable position to avoid dualism and uphold the divine as immanent in creation. They have nature on their side. Far better therefore to avoid a single, good, light, male god up in his heaven and his denied dark counterpart in the world down below, and stay with inclusivity – a sense of the whole. The uncreated *Tao,* the 'Way,' of the East; or *Wakan Tanka*, the 'Great Mystery,' of North America; or the *Mana*, the 'ubiquitous power,' of the Polynesians; or the *Ch'i* or *Ki*, the 'life force,' of the Far East; or the *Dharmata*, the 'Ground Luminosity,' of the Buddhists, are all examples of inclusive alternatives. Or if we are to remain within the terms of the European Tradition then it may help to clothe the sacred in a comprehensive garb. A garb that allows the whole cycle of dark and light, good and evil, to unfold itself within the vocabulary and conceptual thinking that the tradition provides.

Hence: the Goddess and the God. They provide a simple and unequivocal way for consciousness to think about the whole with all of its ambivalent and changing parts. The God and Goddess are doorways to complementary powers that connect all things together. In all their aspects, they are ways of thinking about the self and the divine in which good and evil, dark and light, exist together. They provide a functional cosmology based upon the real, observable polarity of male and female, and which, furthermore, tells the whole story of the creation. Their story makes sense of the sexuality, the life force, the death and chaos of the cosmos. We may add into this archetypically rich alchemical brew the plants, the animals, the trickster, the androgyne, the hermaphrodite, the homosexual, the go-between the worlds. And why not? The unfolding of the genetic impulse requires every form to find its place within the community of life on earth.

So let us come to it with alacrity, if not, I hope, alarm. No, I do not believe in the external nuts-and-bolts existence of God. I do believe the existence of the many aspects of the gods and goddesses in consciousness serves an essential purpose though. It is more than simply useful to know the sanctity and the divine nature of the self and the creation, it is absolutely crucial.

Due to the polarities evident everywhere in the world, the binary nature of thought and language, and the neurological structure of the brain itself, linguistic psychologists tell us that the mind is constantly compensating for itself. The mind registers edible or inedible, friend or foe, fortunate or unfortunate, I or not I, and so on. It follows that a cosmology, which offers a round of choices in the form of metaphorical, allegorical, and analogical thought, will allow its holders to happily flow in the spaces between this binary codification and therefore be at ease within the actual ambiguities and qualifying circumstances of real life. Whereas a cosmology which dogmatically offers only one up there and one down there alternative, will induce a most inconvenient suffering in its believers by virtue of the propensity of language and the mind for equality, balance, and compensation. The more something is reified – given a reality it does not have – the more the thing that is equal and opposite to it comes into being.

The philosopher Ernst Cassirer suggested that when religious speculation denies the distinction between 'subject' and 'object,' between being and self, and thereby arrives at the transcendental, the 'I am that I am' of Jehovah or Allah – a unity and a monotheism way beyond words – the only healthy, yes healthy, alternative which remains to the mind is negation. C. G. Jung also had something on it called the 'Theory of Compensation.' This essentially said you can't beat a warped floorboard down. It will keep popping up at the edges. A messy job.

Belief in a monotheistic, metaphysically irreducible, transcendent, creator God begot a Devil who is everything God is but in the denied realm of the shadow. If you add to this a belief in a physically real, bearded and so on God, then you get a physically real horn-and-cloven-footed Devil. As we live in the created world and not in transcendence, the Devil therefore becomes ubiquitous. He is the "ruler of this world." He rules the realms symbolically identified with him: the body, sex, nature, pleasure, pain, suffering, sickness, death, desire, the feminine, and the dark. The more a discarnate God is pursued the more the incarnate demons catch up from behind. As humans have the ability to bring their beliefs into existence and create in external reality what is in their minds,

94

such a cosmology eventually creates a world of dogma, boundaries, prisons, wars, crusades, *jihads*, intolerance, and very scary demons under the bed. It will also demonise the forests, revile and conceal death and decay, enslave people, deny the body, repress sexuality, denigrate women, and libel perfectly inoffensive and useful carnivores such as coyotes, foxes, wolves and vultures. This is unhealthy.

Through maintaining a light-oriented, monotheistic, and trans-cendent cosmology, a dualism is created whereby good becomes an unattainable absolute outside the world and evil becomes the ubiquitous but denied condition of existence. In the mentality of the adherents of the three main desert religions: Judaism, Chris-tianity and Islam, and in the more fundamental forms of Hinduism and other revealed religions, this is reified into the opposition of God and the Devil. The language for talking about these absolutes becomes impossible. Words can neither describe one nor the other. The divine is outside of creation; the condition of creation is shameful, odious, defiled, and defileable. From out of this situation the dominant male cultures of the world maintain the power they need to sustain themselves. The Devil provides the label for the 'enemy.' The enemy is anyone who does not believe in the reified god. The unbeliever becomes the indescribable 'other,' the infidel, the *kuffar*, those lowest in the caste system. All that is 'bad' can be conveniently projected onto the demonic enemy without or the devilish scapegoat within.

The transcendent God furthermore, provides the means by which a man is allowed to feel privileged, but never privileged enough. The higher he climbs up the hierarchical structure of power toward the light, the shining goal is always out of reach. It, in fact, never can be reached. Like the emperor's new clothes, the distant good, heaven, paradise, and so on, are rarefied to the point of non-existence. The cosmology ends up only sustaining and legitimating the hierarchy of secular power. It maintains the legitimation of the means of control and dominion over others and the natural world. It legitimates even the use of violence to sustain itself. It creates thinking in terms of a duality that maintains asymmetries of race, species, class, age, and gender. It provides no terms to internalise or reconcile differences. Its good-and-evil, take-no-prisoners dualism, separates everything, leaving unity outside of the created world.

The living, immanent symbols of the Gods and the Goddesses are excluded from Western cosmology with alarming effects. They may not be necessary to our thoughts in the long run, but we have not got there yet. While we require a complete pantheon of deities so we can talk about, find relatedness in, and thus understand our inner world, the impossible-to-talk-about dualistic cosmology of God and his projected and denied shadow still predominates in our mentality, and is simply too divisive for our good health.

We stud the inner sky of our minds with images, ideas and concepts on a continuous basis. Some of the ideas we create seem so real and are so powerful that they become apparently autonomous. They have what may be called an archetypal presence within our minds, shared by everyone. The Jungian idea of the 'collective unconscious' is yet to be adequately demonstrated, but it is here, if anywhere, that the archetypal powers we create gather and try and persuade us – succeeding in some cases – that they create us. It is constantly necessary to remind ourselves that we live in a real not an abstract world. The idea of a leopard is not the same as the reality of leopard, although it is still very powerful and may come to haunt us. When the image of the divine is abstracted and removed from the world of real things then the sacred becomes very remote. Its fragmented, idealised parts may appear and suggest impossibilities like messiahship or martyrdom. When the whole round of our existence is constellated within us as immanent presence, and is understood to be revealed in the world of real things, then we will find it easy to move around it, find meaning within it, find relatedness, accept paradox, change and plurality, and express our wholeness.

The Gods and Goddesses are manifestations of our own minds. They stud the starry universe that wheels within and only within our eyes. They work as powerful keys to our experience enabling us to understand the sanctity of the world and our place within it. The monotheistic and transcendent God has proved to be a rather unsuccessful experiment in this exercise. Why would a mind full of Gods, Dark Gods, Goddesses, Light Gods, and Solar Goddesses –

not to mention zoomorphic deities, androgynes, hermaphrodites and tricksters – be any healthier? The kids are going to be just as alienated by a jackal-headed effigy of the God or by a Whipping Kachina as they are of descriptions of the Devil, right? I think not. By allowing the whole round of deity a language and a ritual context to think about the sacred in, by denying or reifying none of them, a rich and enabling means is provided for each individual to meet, process, and internalise the contents of their own being, however dark, as each deity arises and constellates itself uniquely within their consciousness.

Lucifer – The angelic 'Light Bringer' who, in the Judaeo-Christian tradition, falls from heaven for attempting to be like God. Originally a Canaanite Morning Star God heralding the daily birth of the Sun, the prototype of Lucifer as we now know him lies in the attempt by a minor deity to fill the place of the God while he is in the Underworld. In the Canaanite Semitic tradition, Athtar, God of Venus, attempts the role of Baal while he is in the Underworld. In Judaism, such rivalry to God is intolerable and the usurper became the Devil.

In the Celtic tradition Llew or Lugh 'Shining One' is the God of Light, whose rites are held from summer solstice to harvest. The rites include the fertilisation of the Great Earth Mother by the God in the form of a descending lightning-serpent. The rites culminate in a sacred marriage of the Lord of Sexuality and Lightning with the Sovereign Lady of the Land. In the Welsh tradition, Llew dies, undergoes torment, hangs in the branches of an oak tree and is restored as a bringer of language and wisdom. Lucifer may ultimately be restored as the aspect of deity that assists in the growth of the self through the determination and courage to go into the heights and down into the depths. Through the Biblical tradition Lucifer is associated with the serpent and the Sacred Tree.

Sukunyum – To the Lacandon Maya, Sukunyum is the God of the Underworld who carries the dark sun on his shoulders during the night. His Underworld is a beautiful place, inhabited by the night jaguars, richly feathered birds, and prolific trees. Sukunyum guides and advises the souls of the dead.

19

The Devil

The Devil is whatever the concept of him is. If it is a perso-nification of what is perceived in a society as evil, then that personification is the Devil. He has no objective definition, as he has no external existence. Similar concepts of the Devil emerge in historical traditions that share particular mythic symbols.

The dismissal of the dualistic concept of good and evil described in these pages is not a dismissal of evil. Evil does exist. The ability to know that abusing a child, inflicting cruelty upon animals, warring on civilians, or practicing torture, ethnic cleansing and genocide, are evil, is a hallmark of what it means to be a human being. These things are non-negotiable. This does not mean that an absolute duality of good and evil exists, somehow ordained and given to us for our salvation. Nor does it mean that good or evil exist as entities or in people external to us. In fact it is the externalisation and objec-tification of good or evil that is extremely harmful. Telling a suscep-tible person, such as a child, that a 'demon' exists or evil resides among a particular group of people, creates and sustains a worldview of immense irresponsibility.

Underneath the acts of even malicious people is a message that is often quite the opposite. It may even be a love message that has become lost and twisted as a result of abuse, neglect and trauma received as a child. The pain, anger and fear that is felt inside is diffi-cult to integrate when a culture is in collective denial of its own internal shadows or dark side. A person can never integrate those shadows when they are projected externally onto a demon, others, or an enemy. It is often true that, "what we dislike most in others is what we are trying to conceal in ourselves."

By implying that 'evil' is out there as a personification in the world, the members of a culture create a cosmology in which responsibility for personal action or inaction can be denied. This is both on the part of the vociferous upholders of the 'good' of the culture and those who feel ostracised, powerless, and outside the normative structures of the culture. These latter may amplify their self-perceived deviance to the point where they say the 'devil' made them do it, or even that they are possessed by him. They do it to fulfil the values projected onto them. A young teenager for example, never feeling good enough, never having the faith others seem to have, may deliberately exaggerate their deviant actions to gain attention, to shock, or to express his or her own pain. Their actions are a 'fuck you' to society; a, 'if you think that's bad, watch this!' In the rare circumstances where an initial trauma causes a severe psychological dislocation the teenager may internalise the projected demonic imagery of their society, amplify it and exactly manifest it. As, for example in the Salem witch trials, this manifestation will take on the appearance of the cultural conception of the devil. This is taken as providing 'proof' that the devil exists to his prosecutors. It in fact proves nothing but the dangers of impressing upon the vulnerable a world in which good and evil have external objectifications. It certainly has nothing to do with the old earth-focused, mythic and polytheistic spirituality.

Teachings that personify a God and a Devil and so lose sight of the purpose of the many deities to facilitate the transformational journey, can become dangerous as they literalise the mythic, fictional and allegorical qualities of their tradition. Some interpretations of the doctrine of contemporary religions have moved far from mythic allegory and deeply into the literal. God no longer means the all – the dualities, ambiguities, and paradoxes that exist in the world – but an absolute and narrow concept of omnipotent power created by believers. When reified into the structures of human organisation, be it a church, a political party, a terrorist network, or a legal system, it creates totalitarian circumstances, under which the only remaining healthy option for the mind – dissent or disbelief – becomes in itself evil and of the Devil. The upholders of the faith, seeing themselves surrounded by unbelievers or a corrupt world, feel perfectly justified in resorting to violence and war.

The Devil is whatever the concept of him is. If it is a personification of what is perceived in a society, or by a subculture of that society, as evil, then that personification is the Devil. The Devil has no objective definition, as he has no external existence. Similar concepts of the Devil emerge in historical traditions that share particular mythic symbols. We have seen that a male, part animal symbol became this concept in the West as a result of a historical process which reified his opposite, a local deity of light, to a position of transcendent creator. Other circumstances saw this concept become defined in quite another way.

The Eastern tradition for example, sees the demon Mara as that which causes people to bind themselves to the Wheel of Birth, Suffering and Death. Mara is the property of mind that opposes enlightenment. To the Buddhists this is evil. The Western mind might see this as the Devil, but Mara, although personified, is not viewed as being external to the self. Mara is a property of each individual mind. The Western tradition has a long and gruesome tradition that constantly tends toward personification of evil beyond the self. This is not so in the East.

The Devil emerges in the West as the product of dualistic cosmology. The Devil is the 'real' counterpart of a 'real' God. He is that which is denied and projected. At times the symbols of evil become congruent and a strong focus emerges. There may be what is known as a 'Satanic Panic.' The 'Devil' emerges in a particular form in a certain area usually among a disenfranchised – e.g. young, female, minority – class. This is what happened in Salem, Massachusetts. The persecution, repression, intolerance and witch hunts that followed created a real evil which far outweighed the usefulness of retaining the personification of the concept of evil.

In every modern instance where the use of 'Satanic' motifs was verified in a criminal case, investigators did not find proof of the fundamentalist fear that Satan was carrying out his plan to corrupt the world. They found that motifs were taken from religious texts and used for example by members of a group as 'markers' of their psychic and geographic territory. At worst, a dominant and sociopathic individual, such as Charles Manson, uses religious imagery to control and manipulate the members of a group engaged in unlawful activities. The same may be said for manipulators of the motifs of the good external god, such as the extreme tele-evangelists.

Evil is not one part of a personified duality, but is something people do, or do not do, and for which they are responsible. It is evil for example, to deliberately promote and perpetuate division between people, and between people and things. The refusal to examine and own internal thoughts and feelings, and the projection of them outside of the self, might result in evil acts of violence. Evil might be wilful ignorance and the deliberate abuse of power. Evil is the power of someone in authority using the position neglectfully or oppressively. It might result in evil to uphold the structure of privilege and power regardless of the means and content. It might result in evil to fail to fulfil the responsibilities of a social position, or to fail to resist and actively oppose oppression by the powerful. The classic example of the latter in the last century being the failure on the part of the German people to oppose the Nazi concentration camps. Power, of course, need not be just political authority; it may be knowledge, age, gender, race, and strength.

Mara – The Buddhist Lord of Death. Mara, literally the 'death causer,' carries the Wheel of Existence upon which he attempts to bind the soul to repeated rebirth, death and suffering. Mara, as well as the other Hindu and Buddhist Lords of Death such as Yama, Bhairab and Kala, is not the moral focus or personification of evil. He is the property of the individual mind that resists enlightenment. Mara challenged the Buddha many times prior to the realisation of his true nature. He is not always conceived of as a single deity. His mount is the elephant.

Chernobog – The Slavonic 'Black God.' The opposite to Byelobog, the 'White God.' Chernobog is the God of Night and Death. After the introduction of Christianity he symbolised misfortune and evil.

Satan – Strictly speaking not a God, although Satan or Shaytan is shared by the Moslem, Christian and Judaic faiths. In Hebrew,

101

'satan' connotes an adversary of any kind. In late non-scriptural Judaism the word came to mean a being responsible for evil. Evil is defined here as anything which opposes the covenant between the Hebrews, God, and the rule of his representative on earth, the divine king. Christianity adopted this belief. In the New Testament Satan thus became the demonic being opposing God's rule through Christ. Devil comes from the Greek 'diabolos,' which has a dual sense of accuser and obstructer. Among many Moslems, Shaytan means the subtle and overt forces that prevent the establishment of Islamic law. Currently, the 'Great Satan' is the president of the USA. He returns them the sobriquet.

Belief in the corporeal existence of the Devil is suggested by such things as the Gospel of Mark, where Christ drives out demons, by the story of the Temptation, and by the Roman Rite of Baptism, which originally included an exorcism. Writers like Thomas Aquinas believed the Devil capable of having sex with human beings. Such beliefs indicate that Christianity always hovers on the brink of dualism. Christianity has a tendency toward seeing good and evil as primary irreducible forces of existence, but doctrinally comes down on the side of the omniscience of a transcendent good God. In Satan Christians can find a scapegoat for evil whenever the emphasis on monotheism looks like putting too much blame on God. When pushed to explain itself, Christian orthodoxy describes Satan as a negation of good, as an absence of morality, and as 'non-being,' rather than as a separate entity. But in practice many people under the cultural influence of the Desert religions believe in the existence of a corporeal entity that is the personification of evil.

Satan is identified with the serpent and bears horns. He shares these aspects with many Gods of other traditions, e.g. Shiva, Set, Bel, Baal, Dionysos, Loki, and Cernunnos.

20

God of Games

Games are here, now, unrehearsed, unacted, present tense events.
They are a point of connection with life, with wild nature. The
contest, kept fair and equal, pushes the opponents to achieve what
has not yet been achieved. And when kept equal between people,
the contest demands supreme fitness. In their search for the best,
games place their participants on the evolving edge of life.

The God has an aspect that presides over games and competitions of every kind. The Gods and Goddesses in general love the sports arena, and nowhere is this made clearer than in the original Olympic games, named after the Greek pantheon, the Olympians. The games were dedicated to Zeus, the chief of the Olympians, and included not only sports contests, but also artistic, literary, and musical competitions. Of the Greek Gods, Ares loved sports the most, especially when they degenerated into violence. But his equivalent in the Roman pantheon, Mars, had a less aggressive edge. He preferred equal contests and outcomes that led back, eventually, to his original purpose as a God of Agriculture. Roman wars tended to be utilitarian.

As a guardian and protector, Mars was popular with gladiators. In Rome, the priests of the Temple of Bellona, the partner of Mars, were selected from gladiators. The gladiator provides men with an understanding of the ultimate challenge a man can face. It is one thing to hunt a deer in the forest, to pit ones wits against a wild creature, full of flight and survival instinct. It is another thing to hunt a wild boar or a big cat, a creature whose intelligence in attack is so much greater than that of a deer. It is quite another thing to pit ones wits against another man; a man trained in the same arts as oneself, and in the same superb physical condition. This is the contest of the gladiator, and it is the contest sought by the God of Games. He is not interested in unequal or overwhelming odds, in occupation or deceit. He wants to see two or more equally matched men attempt to use every ability at their disposal: mental, physical, emotional and spiritual, to contest each other for greatness and honour.

There is great honour to be won in such equally matched opposition. It tests a man, and brings him and his people to the peak of their abilities. When the great Irish champion Cuchulainn first arrives at the royal seat of Ulster, Emain Macha, a game of hurling is taking place. They are taking place on every subsequent visit we make to Emain Macha. The games, in fact, never cease. At every opportunity in the ancient Celtic world a game of some sort is taking place. It is the backdrop against which life happens, and against which the greatness of a man is measured. Even in the Celtic Otherworld, one of the chief delights is "to behold the plain where the hosts hold their games... where chariots race over the white-silver plain." And, in every Celtic tribe, one God in particular presides over the games.

This God is something of a mystery. He has a name, but to us it appears as the name of a town, an area, or a tribe. If a modern day football supporter in Britain for example was to shout "City!" in the street, you might come closest to the nature of the name and its meaning. Most often, this Celtic God is known as Teutates, literally 'the tribe,' and immortalised forever by the exclamation in the *Asterix* comics, "By Toutatis!" It is the shout of the land on which the tribe dwells. It is the battle cry of the Scottish clansman naming the hill or glen where he was born. It is deep, primal, and if the reader has guessed the writer is being a little tongue in cheek here and will forgive him, it is utterly essential to optimising the flow of life through the veins of the people.

In the Americas, the one thing – other than the stepped pyramid – that the many pre-invasion cultures had in common was the ball court, and with it a ball game. We know little about the game now, but we do know it involved ritualised competition. In Mayan culture for example, the competitors wore highly decorated clothing, and were organised into teams, which, at certain times of the year, engaged in 'flower wars.' Further north, and later in time, Europeans observed highly ritualised games – like lacrosse – involving hundreds of players, that at times celebrated champions and their feats of prowess, and at other times turned into collective prayer. I am sure a City supporter today could empathise. In Europe itself, many games originated in a sacred-spiritual context, or rather they were not seen as isolated from the rest of life. The game of cricket for example contains esoteric imagery, and likewise chess, and other board and card (Tarot) games, are rich in symbolism.

Today, as in the past, we select champions to represent us. The champion in the courts of the Celtic warrior-aristocracy, the champion Samurai of Japan, the champions who have counted most coups against their opponents on the American plains, the champions of the Formula One races and the premier division football clubs, have demonstrated their worth in the genetic stakes and are most likely to have their genes propagated. This is not simply selection through testosterone and physical strength. The contests these opponents practice require peak mental and emotional clarity and incisiveness. It is passing the test that tells them, and us, they are one with the drive that runs through life. And so, perhaps above all, the test of the true champion is about honour. The honour of what it means to integrate every aspect of what we desire most in the God.

The significance of competitive games is that they are here, now, unrehearsed, unacted, present tense events, happening before your face, in this very moment. It is an authentic point of connection with life. It is a point of connection with wild nature, for animals also love the chase, and few Gods and Goddesses of nature are without their hounds, hawks and their horses. The hunt coursing through the brush on a mountainside, horns blowing, flags streaming, is as much a part of the evolving perfection of life, as the elk, the deer, the boar, the horse, and the antelope they are hunting. The contest, kept fair and equal, pushes the opponents to achieve what has not yet been achieved. And when kept equal between people, the contest demands supreme fitness. So today, without the hunt, it is perfect that cities and nations contest each other through sport. It provides the connection with the present moment of life; and in its search for the best, it places its opponents and observers on the evolving edge of life.

Whether it is in cricket or kung fu, football or lacrosse, the God of Games, of life, of the land itself, fuelled by hormones, is driving the contestants to greatness through excellence in every aspect of what it means to be a human being.

Mars – Although the Roman God of War, Mars began life as a local God of Agriculture. He was responsible for the fertility and the safety of fields and their crops. He was a beneficent guardian of the land, of farmers, their barns and buildings. His shield fell from the sky, suggesting lightning or meteoric iron. He was the father of the foundation deities of Rome, Romulus and Remus. His time is spring, and the month of March is named after him. True however to the defender-attacker paradox men so often find themselves in, it was not long before Mars presided over the taking of the crops of others. Mars himself upheld the honour and virtues of war, but his later partners, including Bellona, tended to be vicious and cruel goddesses of blood and gore. In the Greek pantheon the other deities despised Ares for his total love of war, destruction and violence, and as Mars became increasingly identified with Ares, so did his combative functions.

Teutates – Continental Gallic God of the Tribe (*Tuat* or *Tuatha*, 'tribe' or 'people'). If Mars is the aspect of the God who is aggressive in competition, and Ares is his expression taken to its violent extreme in war, then Teutates is the aspect of the God who competes for honour, greatness and glory in contests of skill, courage and fair play. The Celts were shocked when they realised the Romans fought to kill. For many of the Celtic tribes, war was a spectacle where disputes were settled by a contest between champions. The contest might be won through satirising the opponent before a blow was dealt. The first wound was enough to settle any lingering doubts as to where victory lay. It is doubtful that a God called Teutates existed outside of a small region in France. He lives in the name the crowd shout in the stadium. He is the testosterone-fuelled vigour of the people and the land from which they spring.

21

From God of Nature to God of Culture

. . . for a man to become whole, he must look into the fragmentation in consciousness of the mythic image of the divine masculine. He must look into the face of the God — especially its demonic extremes — if he is to reconcile the contradictions engendered between the messages he hears from his own body and those he hears from his culture.

The question, "who is the God?" is answered in part by asking, "what is a man?" Like the God caught in a history of dualism, men are also caught in a double bind. On the one hand men are supposed to be fine, honest, upstanding, and loyal members of their community, tribe or nation, and on the other hand they are supposed to be willing to kill for their community, tribe or nation. Of course it's not put like that. It emerges when honour upon honour is piled upon men killed in military action: "Greater love has no man than when he lays down his life for his friends," and so forth. It still adds up to the same thing. Men are supposed to be honest and ethical, and at the same time are required to kill and be killed upon demand. A strange contradiction is exposed here; a contradiction that few seem willing to look at. For the spectre it raises is that a violent moral code will breed violent men, while the internal definition of a moral society is that men are meant to be peaceful, honest and good.

This contradiction is exposed as early as the 9th Century B.C.E. in the Trojan War. Homer's poetic masterpiece, the *Iliad,* reveals that the very thing those heroic Greeks were afraid of was them-selves. In creating the soldier to defend their walled cities and their beautiful women they were creating the ethos of the warrior who went and attacked those walled cities and captured those beautiful women. The wooden horse, which deceives the Trojans by presenting one thing on the outside and being another on the inside, turns out to be the definition of a man. The horse, like a man, is noble without, yet conceals a murderer within. This looks like the beginning of three thousand years of denial of the dark side of a man and the projection of an unattainable good.

There is more even further back in time however. Although the stories of Achilles, wily Odysseus, and the Trojans are handed down from earlier centuries by oral tradition, the issue has its roots in earlier millennia. The contradiction within the archetypal nature of masculinity and its divine image begins with one of the most massive changes humanity ever went through. This is the transition from nomadic hunter-gatherer to either a settled village agriculturalist or a horse-riding pastoralist.

After an initial phase for humanity lasting several million years, there was a second phase lasting several hundred thousand years. During this epoch, defined as the Palaeolithic, human beings developed an astonishing set of abilities. Our talents excelled in the combination of hand, eye, tool and brain. In this Eden, the proverbial 'Golden Age,' language flourished, the arts, burial rites, and other rites of transition developed. Anthropologists, such as Joseph Campbell, assert that human consciousness saw the world and all that was in it as a whole. There was no differentiation of nature and spirit, and little distinction between the consciousness and identity of the self and that of the tribe. If there was any early image of the sacred during this period it was the 'Great Mother,' the oldest matriarch, through whom all in the tribe were related. This is attested by the cave art and sculpture toward the end of the Palaeolithic era. These major formative events, which shaped the human body and mind, were irreversibly imprinted upon our genes.

By comparison, the final epoch, the last eight or nine thousand years since that huge unbroken length of time are very small indeed. But it is upon entering this epoch that nearly all humanity went through its most dramatic changes. The man in a suit and tie, behind a city desk, is in fact possessed by a set of extraordinary psychosomatic abilities bred for quite another time. His olfactory sense alone is sitting almost entirely unused, probably atrophying, and still it is capable of detecting a creature, say in heat, a mile down wind. The genes have yet to respond to the new set of events and behave themselves. After all, it is a mere 450 generations since the beginning of the changes (assuming twenty years a generation), less than fifteen generations since the earliest industrialisation, while our ancestors spent at least 20,000 generations in 'Eden' and many times that in getting there.

The evidence is fractured, broken. The windows on the past are obscured, tiny, and always tinted by our perspective, but a view exists nonetheless. Perhaps the best view of the original Eden is found in reports by travellers before the onslaught of Western culture who describe hunter-gatherers as dwelling in a world of essential unity. A spirit, it is reported, that is not separate from the indwelling spirit of the individual or the tribe, animates everything. Moreover, this spirit is sacred, and the energies of the members of the tribe are mostly directed into activities that support it. After subsistence needs are met – a few hours a day – they devote their time to myth, storytelling, and ritual, for example, the making of elaborate paraphernalia for a rite of passage or for the marking of a turning point in the cycle of the seasons. The people involve themselves, anthropologists say, in "full dramatic participation" within the cycle of life. The cosmologies and stories of creation tell of the communion of all things and the integral place and role of humans in existence. Psychologists inform us that contained within and produced by such a worldview lies a deep sense of purpose, relatedness, comprehension, and meaningfulness.

The trauma came with the changes. Humanity was taken from one existence into quite another through the process of settlement, urbanisation, domestication of animals and agriculture. Women appear to have adapted remarkably better than the men. Perhaps the transition was not so difficult because women's activities already centred on hearth and home. Perhaps women encouraged or were in some way partly responsible for the transition. Men on the other hand faced an enormous challenge. The part of them that had found purpose and relatedness in the extremely ancient traditional way of life went unsatisfied. There was no longer the hunt, the shamanic or mystical sense of communion with the big game. There was no longer the nomadic cycle of movement, or a meaningful place for the ritual cycle of men's activities, nearly all of which took place in wild nature. Men's activities became a function either of an agricultural urban culture or of a pastoral economy. The choice between the two was determined by geography. The rich soils of Europe lent themselves to agriculture, while the plains of central Asia encouraged the development of the pastoral horse-culture.

In Neolithic Europe (9,000 – 2,000 B.C.E.), men were turned in upon the fixed settlement, the domestic crafts, the fields and the water sources – all of which were in the domain of women. The Neolithic agricultural revolution put power and authority into the hands of women. Representations of the Great Mother Goddess proliferate from this time. She is the creative source of life. She is shown as the sprouting seed, the fruits of the field, the womb of birth, the granary, the oven, the storehouse, and the tomb of rebirth. The far fewer images of the male remain in the realm of nature, as animal, or as a phallus. The divine masculine role became that of the son and the lover of the Great Goddess.

The result of this enormous cosmological shift was that male energy could not be directed in the traditional and long-established ancestral manner. Men became the ploughers of the female-identified field, the sowers and reapers of the female-identified grain, the makers and defenders of the female-identified irrigation canal, the herders of the female-identified cattle. Society was endogamous, matricentric, communal, temple building, and Earth Goddess-worshipping. The emerging image of the God was as the spirit of vegetation and of animals, seasonally rising and falling between the worlds, in the role of 'consort' to the Goddess.

The changes went in entirely the opposite direction on the pastoral steppes. Here women did not do so well. Society became patrilineal, exogamous, hierarchical, and Sky God-worshipping. The Indo-European people of central and western Asia developed a dualistic image of God – a God of Light and a God of Dark, one identified with good and one with evil. The Solar God of the vast plains fought only with the night. Otherwise the sun always remained the same. The European Goddess-focused communities had no such concern, seeing all in terms of the lunar cycle of regeneration. But on the steppes the Earth Goddess came to passively depend upon the powers of the Sky God for her fertility. The horsemen of the steppes developed weaponry far beyond those needed for hunting. Their mobility meant a long and gradual incursion into the agricultural communities to the south and to the west.

Between 3,000 and 1,500 B.C.E. Indo-European culture swamped the Near East, Eastern Europe, and the Indus Basin. Its pastoral economy, language, patriarchal ideas, and warrior ethos proliferated at the expense of the matricentric agricultural communities. Rules of exogamy (marrying outside the clan) were laid down. This was directly aimed at the old endogamous societies in which brother and sister were equals and, at least in mythology, co-rulers and often mates. Whether sibling-marriage happened or not, incest rules ended the endogamous (in-marrying) character of matricentric society.

We can guess however that neither developmental extreme quite satisfied the ache in men for the ancient way of life. This was neither matricentric nor patricentric, although the image of the Great Mother ultimately contained the potentials of both. Men were torn between the emerging mythic images of the sacred masculine. The image of the God as son and lover of the Goddess, he who journeyed around the whole cycle of her existence, became divided. The God was now either a God of the Earth and the Underworld, or a God of the Heavens. The two fought each other, and the God of Light, of good, eventually triumphed. Evil was projected externally, onto the enemy, their gods and, in some cases, onto women.

We saw above in the example from Homer how Greek men came to be the defenders of the female-identified towns from their own oppression. In the story of Troy, where the culture fused elements of both the indigenous European and the Indo-European traditions, all the paradoxes rolled into one. It was the women who wanted their sons to be the fighters who defended them from the fighters. The archaic yet sexually liberated matriarchate of Sparta found fulfilment, almost apotheosis, in the return of their sons from battle, dead upon a shield. A contradiction was generated that is not resolved to this day. A contradiction moreover further from consciousness now than it ever was. Attempts were made in antiquity, especially in the stable land of Egypt, to find a role for the divine masculine that fully incorporated his nature. This included co-rule of brother and sister, and teaching upon the essential unity of good and evil, personified by Osiris and Set. But today, as a result of centuries of domination by the Light God of the patriarchal Church and State, and now secular materialism – with the Goddess-folk-religion fomenting as ever at the edges – the situation is no better, possibly worse.

The contradiction is not resolved by blaming men. As for example in the currently popular interpretation of prehistory where the aggressive patriarchal hordes sweeping down upon the peaceful matriarchal villages are all to blame. The implication being that the male character, if allowed to gain the upper hand, is the cause of everything bad. History rarely admits to simple moral explanations like this. In truth, the move to settled agriculture in Europe and pastoralism in Asia, and the subsequent story of acculturation, encroachment and invasion, is a complex patchwork quilt involving many factors, very different areas, and many millennia. If the men-to-blame interpretation is insisted upon, then an opposite case could be made which places equal culpability upon the women. For example, urban culture-creating women tore men away from their earth-honouring and vision-seeking natural harmony and enforced the tyranny of the womb with its laws of blood for blood, and so on. Although it is true we are emerging from a long period of patriarchal domination – the Sky God-worshipping Indo-Europeans *did* get the upper hand – the tendency to power, or to good or evil, is neither a sole prerogative of men or women.

Men were, and still are, desperate for meaning in this new world order. They sought any cosmology or rationalisation that made sense of the world. Bringing their millennia aged sensibilities of the hunt to war for example, they sought to make it honourable. The test of courage, the battle of equal champions, as recorded by the Celts, the Polynesians, the Sioux, the Chinese, the Japanese, and so on, indubitably was honourable. But throughout the last few thousand years war for most of these cultures has not been so. The image of the divine masculine remains divided. The male psyche became and still is fragmented. It does not know which way to turn. In the new urban or pastoral order of Eurasia it became impossible for men to sense their role within the cyclical whole. The linear cosmological doctrine of the transcendent creator god of light and goodness and the chthonic god of evil became increasingly absolute. It even provided a way to make sense of it all. A man could attribute the good in himself to God and the trauma of the changes to the 'other,' to Satan, and to sin.

If this interpretation has any truth to history, then it follows that for a man to become whole, he must look into the fragmentation in consciousness of the mythic image of the divine masculine. He must look into the face of the God – especially its demonic extremes – if he is to reconcile the contradictions engendered between the messages he hears from his own body and those he hears from his culture. A contradiction in which his somatic, sexual impulses are strong, vigorous, wild, integral with life, and chthonically spiritual, while the cultural impulses insist upon domestication, obedience, separateness from life, and spiritual transcendence. A contradiction in which the members of a culture – including women – actually want him to be privileged, powerful and brutal, while his deeper self is telling him: "This doesn't make sense! It is against life!"

A resolution of these contradictions could mean the transformation of establishment religion, of military service (in the prevailing political conditions), of patriarchal government, of consumer or market capitalism, of gender and racial oppression, and probably the transformation of the nuclear family as men refuse to participate in them any further. At the risk of sounding facetious, as most of this is below consciousness, if there is no wish to change any of these things then it might be best for society as a whole to remain in collective denial about the meanings it upholds regarding the archetypal nature of men and the God.

Baal – The title Baal or 'Lord' was given to many regional gods of the Near East. In Phoenicia Baal, or Ba'al, was a horned fertility and weather God. To the Philistines Baal was a God of fertility and prophecy. Among the Canaanites Baal reigns throughout the winter months bringing rain, thunder and lightning. In summer, the time of drought, Baal is summoned to the Underworld and slain by the serpent, ocean-current God Mot. The God Athtar, Venus, attempts to take his place, but proves inadequate to the task. Baal's sister-lover, the Goddess Anat, (or the related Goddess Astarte, Asherah or Ashtaroth, 'Lady') searches and grieves for him. She restores him to life. She extracts revenge by cutting, winnowing, grinding and parching Mot to death. This corresponds to the time of harvest in late July. Baal is thus identified with the cycle of vegetation and fertility. He, like Adonis and Tammuz, is a Dying and Rising God.

Baal is represented as a striding warrior. His cult animal is the bull. Baal and Mot may be seen as Dual Gods of the Underworld. They stand in contradistinction to El, the Creator, and God of Heaven. From about 1500 B.C.E. it appears that Yahweh, the Baal of the Israelites, became the monotheistic god of the Hebrews, while Milkom, the Baal of Amman, and Chemos, the Baal of Moab, and so on, became the montheistic god of those regions. Archaeological finds suggest that each region had its own form of monotheism, and that monotheism arose to assist in the unification of small nation-states. The many gods had much in common. Like the Baal of the Canaanites and the other regions, Yahweh struggles with a serpent, Leviathan, brings a world-destroying flood, and dwells in specific shrines. With the political emergence of Israel the other Baals of the region became 'Dark Gods.'

Giants – The Giants are included here with the Gods as they share a common fate. Both are denied a presence in the world. In nearly all traditions the Giants begin their story as assistants in the creation of the world. Their actions and their bodies form the features of the landscape. The Giant Purusha of India, the Giant Ymir of Scandinavia, the Giant P'an Ku of China, and the Giant Gayomart of Persia, form the world and the firmament from out of their bodies. The Titan Prometheus is described as the helper, even the creator of humankind. Then new deities arise, there is a War in

Heaven, and the Giants are banished into the Underworld. The Giants become everything the culture fears, that is, monstrous, cannibalistic, stupid, wild, hostile, and identified with the uncontrollable forces of nature. The Giants, like the Gods, define culture by becoming the 'Other.' They become everything that is outside of culture, which, in this case unfortunately includes the natural world.

Universal myths then describe the defeat of the various Giants: David kills the Canaanite Giants including Goliath, Jack is the Giant Killer, Beowulf crushes Wendel, George kills his Dragon, Zeus imprisons Prometheus. Although this outlook may have a function in transcendentally oriented consciousness, in the world-view of wholeness the Giants represent an important link between humans and the natural world. The Giants are a way of thinking about the earth. Their presence makes the creation immanent and personal. Their present status is a symbol of human estrangement from the world.

Typhon – In Classical mythology, the Giants are born of the Earth Goddess Gaia as a result of the mutilation of her lover the Sky God Uranus by their son, the Titan Cronos. After the Gods and Goddesses of Olympus defeat the Giants and the Titans, they make their dwelling in the Underworld. Gaia, in rage at their defeat, lay with Tartarus to create an even more formidable opponent in the form of the monstrous Typhon. Typhon has wings, the arms and legs of serpents and eyes of fire. He succeeds in defeating and capturing Zeus in his coils. He is only overcome when the mountains he hurls rebound upon him. His fire belches from the earth in volcanoes. Typhon is the father of Cerberus, the Hydra and the Chimaera. He is kin to the serpent Tiamat, Python, Mot, Apep and Adanc. They personify the violent and apparently hostile forces of nature.

Wild Man – The Wild Man of the Northern European tradition has an unkempt, shaggy, green and leafy aspect. In folk tradition he has many names, including Jack in the Green, Fynoderee and Wood-wose. He may appear covered in leaves at festivals, and, like a

115

tree, is struck down to ensure regrowth. He is closely related to the Wild Herdsman, the Lord of the Animals and the Dying and Rising Gods of Vegetation. Adonis, Attis, Tammuz and Osiris all underwent birth or rebirth within a tree. The Wild Man is also related to the Green Man, but their aspects are somewhat different.

The Wild Man appears as guardian of a treasure, which requires a test to receive. In the case of the British Magician Merlin, the test meant becoming a Wild Man. For several years Merlin lived with the animals in the forest. From this he gained his wisdom. The Green Man is an aspect of this wisdom. The Green Man is the mouth through which the Earth Wisdom speaks. He has entered the earth, the Underworld. He has died – connected with the raw chthonian energy of death and vegetation. It gushes forth from his mouth as inspiration. The Wild Man is a more general expression of this unity with the earth, whose potential – in natural wisdom, animal power, wild growth, or Dionysian abandonment – can be tapped and expressed at any moment.

22

The New Cosmology of the God

The purpose of the many deities, be they the European, the Hindu, or the Tibetan pantheon of deities, the Aboriginal ancestors of the Dreamtime, or the American Kachinas, is to facilitate the transformational journey around the infinite contents of the Universal Mind.

The native traditions of Europe, preserved in literature, folklore and archaeology, show that the many different aspects of the God were once recognised and honoured. The traditions reveal that the God symbolised the qualities of the masculine in terms of the transformational cycle of the seasons regardless of whether society was dependent upon the hunt or upon agriculture.

In summary, the domain of the God lay not only in growth, fertility and wealth, but also in the waning year, death, and the Underworld. The God symbolised and provided a connection with an extremely deep source of chthonic, masculine power. As the Wild God, he was the hunter, as well as the Protector of Animals and the Guardian of Nature. Sometimes he is in a terrible, or an animal or phallic form. As the God of Wisdom, the few representations that exist from the early Neolithic phase of European settlement and agriculture – the 8th to 5th millennium B.C.E. – show him either standing, carrying a pruning hook or reaper, or in a seated, inward-looking pose. As the God of the Tree, he was one with life. In all these early instances, it is evident the power comes from within, from nature, and is linked with the seasonal cycle of change.

A graphic living example of this God in all his aspects is Shiva. In India, Shiva is the god of death, fertility, sexuality, the dance, animals, the serpent, and of demons. Through the annihilating dance of Shiva the cosmos is brought to extinction, yet is mercifully preserved and recreated. Among the Gods of the European Celts, Cernunnos is represented like Shiva as a horned, cross-legged deity, holding a snake. Cernunnos is surrounded by animals, by the leaves of the forest, and sometimes has a stream of (golden?) coins flowing from a bag in his lap. Although little is known about Cernunnos, the comparison with the current practices surrounding Shiva is a useful one to make. The antlered and phallic god of fertility, wealth, and the dance, is the oldest represented European male deity; and indeed he is still alive in such traditions as the Abbots Bromley Horn Dancers in Britain. Another form of the Celtic God of the Underworld is Math. He is a god of justice, of wealth, and a teacher of magic. Likewise, the Roman Underworld gods such as Dispater, Hades and Pluto, were originally seen as a benevolent chthonic deities. They provided wealth and fertility, offering up the secret treasures of the earth. This is the classic role of the God. In Japan, the God of the Underworld, Jizo or Kshiti-garbha, is a compassionate guide to the dark realms. He heals and helps the suffering as they pass through his domain.

Later, there is significant literary evidence from Bronze Age and Iron Age cultures that describe the God alternating between the Underworld and the human world. Adonis, Attis, Tammuz, and Dumuzi from the Near East for example, spend half the year in each. They are gods of seasonal fertility. This may be the meaning of the Neolithic seated male figurines. The year is done, and the God of Vegetation is contemplating the journey to the Underworld. Then there are instances where the Light God and the Dark God divide the cycle of the year between them. They are the God of the Waxing Year and the God of the Waning Year. They are born from the Great Goddess and pursue the Great Round of existence as twins and lovers of the Earth Mother. Eventually, like the phases of the moon, they become combatants giving way to each other in an appropriate manner at the appropriate time. As alternating or dying and rising gods they inspired the rich myths of eternal return, the sense of masculine unity with the feminine-identified flux of life, and the inability of humans to hold on to and promote any idea, project, dynasty, or artificial succession, regardless of nature. Examples include Osiris and Set in the Egyptian tradition, Queztalcoatl and Tezcatlipoca in the Aztec, the twin sons of Spiderwoman in the Hopi, Gwynn and Gwythyr in the Welsh tradition, and the Oak and Holly Kings in the British.

Almost everywhere before the Light, Sky, and Solar God gained the upper hand, the God is honoured as guardian and a guide to, or Lord of the Underworld. The powerful figure of Masau was the God of Death and the Underworld in the Third World of the Hopi. Now, in the Fourth World, he is their guide and protector. Sukunyum, the Underworld god of the Lacandon Maya, carries the sun on his shoulders through the night. He helps people in his beautiful realm of forest, animals and flowers to find their truth. The Great Lord Yama, God of the Underworld in Hinduism and Buddhism, is the benevolent God of Death. He guides the soul on its journey through his judgements. Anubis in Egypt plays a similar role. In many traditions, the God greets the soul at the entrance to the Underworld, guides or ferries them across it, and helps the suffering with his wisdom and protection. Wepwawet in the Egyptian tradition, the wolf headed god, is the 'opener of roads.' He guides the boat of Ra and that of the dead through the Underworld.

None can escape the dance of Shiva, the judgement of Osiris, Anubis, Yama and Math. Yet, as always, they give way, and the continued turning of the cycle means the rebirth of their twin, the summer season, or the human soul.

It is easy to see how, for many, the Lord of the Waxing Year – the God of Light – came to be preferred. The return of spring, the fullness of summer, the warm days of harvest are irresistibly attractive. Yet without the field lying fallow, without the frost breaking down the soil, without the dormancy of the trees, without the fertilisation and germination of the seed in the darkness, without the whole cycle of regeneration, none of the harvest is possible. This is represented in cultures with a comprehensive lunar symbology by the three nights of no moon preceding the new moon. Cultures whose cosmology includes reincarnation generally hold the part played by the Underworld God as essential for the transformational journey of the soul.

119

Three nights is the symbolic amount of time spent in a journey to the Underworld.

The Christian cycle of Easter recognises all of this. Without death the resurrection would be impossible. There is mention in the Bible of a three-day visit to the Underworld. But where the earthy, vestigially pagan, beauty of the Christian symbols of Easter begin to break down is where death as an aspect of the God is eternally defeated. Christ dies and rises in the tradition of the prehistoric and Bronze Age Gods, but not as part of the regenerative cycle of life, but once and for all. He is said to utterly destroy the powers of darkness, denying a part to the other half of existence.

And so, under these circumstances, we saw how the God rapidly became the Devil, how the Underworld and its transformational power are closed, and the Goddess was banished. The sexual, procreative power of the Goddess as Earth Mother was removed, and she became asexual or a virgin. The fulfillment provided by the archetypal mythic images of union between God and Goddess vanishes. The body, sex, women as progenitors, the forests, the creatures and the night were reviled. Anger, lust, sexual desire, jealousy – all the inherent 'dark' emotions – are, at this point, doomed. Of course, they – along with human evil – don't go away. Denied within, we saw how they were and continue to be projected outside of the culture, sustaining the dualistic hell. Traumatised and traumatising, every denied human feeling and instinct perpetuates the cycle of abuse when there is no place for its assimilation within the worldview. The hell of evil is sustained when there is no way of talking about it within the black and white cosmology of the culture. The question begged by this summary is of course, where do we go from here?

Contrary to what we were taught in science class, the sun, moon, planets, and stars turn around our world. Our native myths of creation are explicit on this point. First there came the earth, and then, from out of the earth, came the sun and moon. The earth, the stories say, is our mother. It is at the centre of life.

If we took this geocentric myth at face value, a quite different attitude toward the earth would replace the one that currently prevails. The heliocentric, light-oriented, individualistic, transcendent emphasis makes us forget we are all united in a common, chthonic, genetic origin. A geocentric emphasis is especially appropriate in an age where newly emerging scientific paradigms express awe at the complexities, interdependence, subtlety, sophistication, and sublime beauty of the earth and its life forms. Science is arriving at the place where it can only describe the mundane, everyday miracle of life as sacred. The new science shows how the universe resonates within itself on every level; it really does lie within a grain of sand.

Scientists however, whether biologists, physicists, geneticists, or ecologists, agree that they cannot agree on what on first glance appears to be an obvious thing, and that is a definition of life, or of sex for that matter. We don't know what life is. Life and sex consistently elaborate themselves away from any theory that would frame them. The apparently irrefutable fact of a discrete entity, such as a human being, crumbles away when it is realised that there is no cell in the human body that did not evolve billions of years ago in quite another form and is present now in many other life forms. The human body might be said to be one exercise in many that are testing the cooperative abilities of cells. Cells more-over, that are quite capable of scrapping the whole experiment and starting again.

The point here is that human beings share with all other living beings a genetic, cellular, information network. This is a rich, diverse, multiform, composite body extending throughout the atmospheric, solid, and oceanic strata of the earth. The unique capacity of human beings to be self-conscious does not mean separateness from this creative self-sustaining matrix. It implies a responsibility to be self conscious of all of its relationships within it. This is the job of humans, and it is here that we find a high moral purpose. It is not a purpose focused upon scratching through the bin of personal salvation in an effort to attain sinlessness. It is not the fulfillment of self-actualisation, self-directiveness or enlightenment. It is the fulfill-ment of being an integral part of the living community of all beings. This is where the image of the sacred as Earth Goddess is exact. Life comes forth from her and returns to her. Unlike the Creator God outside the world, the Earth Goddess is life. She is not separate from it. Life really does emerge from within, from this moment, not from some distant source event twelve billion light years away. And finally, life sustained through the loving sexual union of male and female as symbolised by the partnerships of the many aspects of God and Goddess, places us on the creative and growing edge of existence.

The moral commitment to good or evil in the context of our watchful consciousness are standards by which we observe and measure the degree of harmony and unity within the ongoing cellular membrane of the life force on planet Earth. Are we on the wave or off it? Is Hans Solo finally going to get the Force or not? Are his actions going to increase or diminish the diversity, quantity, and quality, of the local bioregion? Will he recognise the necessity of many truths and points of view or try to impose a rule of absolute truth? Will the justice he brings connect all together in the web of life or reduce everything to separately evaluated parts? A geocentric philosophy, or a morality of life, might begin to think in these directions.

In fact, a whole new functional cosmology is required. A story of creation is needed that links everything, all of life, together again. The new creation-centred mythology calls for a world in which every being is a welcome and valued part of the community. The focus departs from individual sin, linear time, and transcendental salvation and is placed upon the immanence of the sacred within the cycles of creation.

Here we find that the creation is the revelation of the divine. The focus is upon the earth community and the fulfilment of every creature as a fully incarnated being within it. The focus is not in the future, on what we may become in the next life. The focus is upon the reinternalisation, the geocentrifying, of all human emotions. A moral sense is restored based upon the health, rights, and well being of all life on earth now. Reclaiming the deep, dark, inner realms and so reconciling the split in our consciousness as a result of the mythic fragmentation of the Goddess and the Light and Dark Gods is a necessary step toward this.

The contribution of the God to a new cosmology is that it is precisely he who walks through the messiness of cellular exchange, the sloppiness of sex, and the vital processes of death and decay.

Whether it is in the bacteria in the stomachs of animals, in the micro-organisms on the floor of the forest, or in the top few inches of the soil, the God is there. It is he who provides guidance through all that works below the surface of the earth – the creative but chaotic domain of the Goddess. It is he who actively seeks, separates, quests, even conquests, through the journey of the seed in the sexual genetic pool of life. The presence of the God in the working depths of our psychosomatic being allows a full communion with and a passage through this side of life. For example, anyone who has ever farmed the land or built upon it knows that the place to begin is in the Underworld. It is with the foundations, with the drains and the basic services. If the unseen foundations and drains of a culture are not working then that culture is not working. Its fields become full of a monocrop of ungrounded ideas; they lack roots and choke in the stagnant matter of their own denial.

If we are short of a full and adequate theory, or simply a way of talking about the realm of life and death, then an unavoidable human need is not being met. The same is also true for sex, lower bodily functions, and dealing with the deep-seated, painful, grieving, excruciating, passions of life. Nothing can ever be let go of. Nothing can ever die to be reborn. In ancient Egypt the story of Osiris, God of Death and Life, provided a way of talking about these things. Osiris is imprisoned and dies. His lover Isis revives him. He rises and falls like the Nile. He is slain again and dismembered into fourteen parts. Then he is reconstituted again by her love. He becomes the fertile ground out of which rises the grain crop of the land.

In the Tibetan Buddhist tradition an extremely thorough study of the death and dying process exists. The process is met with at every level of life, and in this case, includes a theory of the afterlife and reincarnation. In the different transitional states known as Bardos, the character of each being's mind, which is determined by their karma, is, as it were, played out in their experience. A recently deceased person, for example, will experience the archetypal re-enactment of the contents of their mind without the buffering effect of the body. This takes the form of the appearance of paradisiacal and hell realms, benevolent and wrathful deities, or what we in the West would call Light and Dark Gods. Now the Tibetans are careful to point out that these experiences are creations of the mind. At any point the deceased may realise this. It is then possible to merge with an experience lying beyond the mind – and really only attainable at death – known as the Dharmata or the 'Ground Luminosity.'

The Wrathful Deities, Yama or Mara, the Lord of Death, or Kala or Mahakala, the destructive form of the Hindu Shiva, constellate themselves according to the unique personalities of the bearers of their cultural tradition. Yama has many arms, a belt of skulls, a gore filled mouth and so on, to those of the Tibetan Buddhist tradition. In Europe however, this aspect of the God may array himself as all or partly animal, as a horned and lusty giant, as a shaggy or leaf-clad elemental, or as a disgorger of leaves. In other words, he may appear as the Horned God, the Green Man, Dionysus, Pan, the Marvel Comic Swamp Thing of the Native European Tradition.

It does not really matter how they appear. The purpose of the many deities, be they the European, the Hindu, or the Tibetan pantheon of deities, the Aboriginal ancestors of the Dreamtime, or the American Kachinas, is to facilitate the transformational journey of each individual around the infinite contents of the Universal Mind.

Horned God – See Cernunnos, Dionysos, Wild Man, and Pan. A widespread and extremely ancient deity. His primary role is that of Guardian of Nature, of fertility, sexuality and the wild forces of growth. When the power of the Horned God flows, those who feel it cannot control themselves and abandon themselves to ecstasy. The full moon shines from the top of his horns, the dark moon at their base. His attributes eventually became those of the aggressive patriarchal warrior cults, such as the 'beserkers' of Odin. But as guardian, protector and herdsman, the Horned God teaches how to nurture the wild creative energies of nature, to increase them for the benefit of all life.

Jizo – Japanese God of the Underworld. Jizo is a compassionate God who conducts and protects souls on their journey after life.

He also protects children, travellers and women. As a Buddhist God of Compassion Jizo assists all suffering beings.

Nodens – British God of the Underworld. Husband of Gwyar, 'gore,' and father of Gwynn ap Nudd. Nodens or Nudd is closely associated with the River Severn. He is a god of the waters, of healing, and of wealth. The main animal of his cult is the dog, guardian of the entrance to the Underworld. He is related to the Irish Nuadha and to the British River God Llud.

Pluto – or Ploutos, is the Roman God of Wealth, born of the Corn Mother Demeter after she lay with Iasion on land that had been 'thrice-ploughed.' He was identified with, and probably is an aspect of Hades, God of Death and the Underworld. Pluto means 'wealthy' or 'rich' and signifies the treasures to be gained from opening the earth.

23

The Whole Image of the God

The journey of the God is deep into the infinite fractal recesses and cycles of nature as well as into the vastnesses of space. He provides the knowing that all is in transition, all must change, and all will come to an end. The God reveals it is possible to change one's mind, to take another path, to let go, to laugh, to cry, to hold on to nothing, and to give everything away. He shows that at the limit of every theory there is another waiting to burst forth. The God demonstrates the mystery of the cutting of the ripened grain, the picking of the fruit, the finality of ejaculation, the closing of the womb after birth, the ending of the year, the sealing of the tomb, the dark of the moon.

Although the Western mind has succeeded in spreading its transcendental, literalist and monotheistic attitudes around the world, the many dimensional mythic God still has a place. It is said in India for example, that more shrines are dressed and more offerings made to Shiva than to any other deity in the world. It is the many aspected God who originated in the several cultural streams that form the European world that has been suppressed.

The suppression was in evidence at the time of the Classical Greeks and Romans. Dionysos was already deemed an outsider. The ruling class disapproved of his rites. Hades was the third-ranking brother of Zeus and Poseidon. Hades and Dionysos were considered fit only for the agricultural and working classes. Today, only the sensational, and hugely exaggerated, aspects of Dionysos are dwelt upon, while Hades is reduced to a rapist. The proper place for Hades wife, Persephone, is felt not to be with him in the Underworld but with her mother, Demeter. Even in Egypt Osiris came to be the God of the working people, while royalty celebrated the Sun God, Ra. Freyr, the Germanic god of fertility, was slain by a Sky God, and his phallic rites and those of his sister-consort Freya, were demonised. The Hebrew prophets castigated Baal. The rites of the country dwellers, the pagans, were ridiculed and despised. So thorough is the intolerant hegemony of the solar and transcendent God, it is likely we have to view back several thousand years in the Western world to gain a glimpse of the mythic God.

Why does this matter? Why is it important to restore the multi-dimensional image of the God? And exactly what, or who, is he?

As has been discussed, the God is an interior presence within the mind. He is an image manifested by individual human conscious-ness. He, like the Goddess and other archetypal images, is a symbol that is present within consciousness. When envisioned and enhanced through the power of complex patterns of myth and symbol, his power actualises itself within the self. He constellates himself for each person uniquely. He has no external existence, but his shared archetypal, symbolic and transpersonal qualities mean he has enormous influence upon external reality when projected onto it. When projected literally, and not figuratively as a function of individual consciousness, the mind tends to maintain the projection outside of itself, that is, it holds it as a collectively agreed upon pattern of beliefs and symbols. In this case, the God and his aspects are assumed to have a real, external existence, which become greater as his temples, rituals, images, codes and doctrines proliferate. This can lead to dogma, which in turn can lead to scapegoating, persecution, forced conversion and discrimina-tion as people are coerced to believe in a prescribed figure of a God. At this point individual spiritual experience is not considered valid, and all depends on the revelation of the spiritual by the few, usually long dead, leaders.

We noted however, that when spiritual experience is self-validated and recognised as a unique interior presence within the mind, albeit with archetypal transpersonal qualities, the result can be completely different. The powerful symbols of deity meet with, enable and allow understanding of individual spiritual experience, generating further growth and personal transformation. The God – and Goddess – can be enormously facilitative of journeys into every dimension of being. The images of deity bring meaning to profound spiritual experiences, and, when allowed many symbolic aspects, they help to reinternalise and integrate the complex experiences of life. They can especially help to integrate challenging experiences that are usually externalised or denied. Perhaps above all, the experience of ultimate and all-encompassing divinity can inspire the individual to goodness, to love, to the increase of intense moral commitment, and to a life of seeking universal well being. Clearly this experience of God, of Goddess, or of any archetypal divine image, cannot be defined, and indeed will suffer from any attempted monopoly of definition.

The traditional epiphanies of the mythic God in all his aspects – as the God of healing, of nature, of the underworld, of the animals, the trees and forests, of compassion, of fertility and abundance – are inclusive and immanent. He can be anywhere. His presence and power can be felt in anything. The God – or Goddess – of sovereignty for example, tells us about our own sovereignty. The God of healing opens up our intuition and logic around healing. Allowing the divine presences into our lovemaking stimulates our ability to love. The God of wealth, tells us about our own wealth. The Dark God tells us about our deep and troubling emotions. Before we continue, it is important to keep in mind that the terrifying or dark aspects of both God and Goddess are not in and of themselves evil. They have no real, external existence and manifest to reveal aspects of ourselves to ourselves. As it is only the things humans chose to do, or not do, that are evil, the moral evaluation of evil attached to many of the Gods described in this book becomes an external projection that can disassociate us from a side of our nature, which, possibly more than any other side, needs careful examination, acknowledgment and integration.

It may be that the imagery and symbolism of the God – and Goddess – may be too negatively loaded, given the prevalence of established religion in the experience of most people in the Western world. It is very easy to slip into the inherited literal thinking of

'God and the Other.' It is easy to forget that the Dark and Light God duality is a distinction arising from a set of particular historical circumstances. It is easy to forget that the concept of the evil God arose with the predominance of the good God, and that everything contrary to the nature of the patriarchal good God was then externalised and projected onto the God. It need not of gone this way of course, but that is what happened in the history of the Western world. It may therefore be necessary to look beyond the historically ingrained opposition of light and dark, good and evil in the symbology of the God, and find sets of mythic symbols which do not provoke reaction.

It may be of most value to look beyond even the archetypal images of Classical mythology – the Greek, Roman and Egyptian pantheons – to the extremely early time when the God, as a whole, underwent the journey around the cycle of creation as son and lover to the Goddess. He rose and fell in harmony with the cycles of life and death. The waxing, waning, full, and dark phases of the moon are a fine expression of his wholeness. The late Palaeolithic, the Neolithic, and the Bronze Age eras provide good examples of this God. He is not a creator. He is not a life-giver. He is not omnipotent. He does not combat evil. Nor does he take life or heroically defeat death. He is a way of thinking about masculine energy that sees it fully participating within the natural cycle of life and death. He provides the means by which men can enhance and increase the seasonal cycle of fertility, can add their energy to it, while simultaneously undergoing the transformations the cycle brings. The Celts inherited much of this view, as described in section 2, *Guide to the Underworld*.

In this view, the God in all his aspects, as Earth God, Dark God, Wise God, Animal God and so on, is the provider of the means by which it becomes possible to name, talk about, and thus find the way around the deeper side of human nature. This enabling God is 'good to think.' The God gives the courage to be ground into the dark earth like the grain. He gives the courage to let go of restraints and inhibitions. He is the guide through the underworld of the more difficult and subconscious thoughts and emotions. Instead of pushing aside grief, loss, death, derangement, pain, anger, fear,

129

passion, ecstasy, wildness and overwhelming desire, he provides the means to go into them. The God gives a voice to humour, contrariness, mischievousness, libidinous energy, lust, jealousy and, if necessary, aggression. His most extreme aspects may mean he will aid the warrior in the deadliest of situations. He will bring up and focus the power of the red serpent lying in the depths of earth. By giving it a form, by giving it a name, the God does not allow this deadly power to get out of hand. Libidinous, bull-like, hormone-driven, red aggression is only blind when denied as an internal aspect of humanity. Allowed back into the reaches of consciousness, it has a use, and those who feel it can turn away from any action that compromises their moral commitment.

If that is not enough, the God may also appear as the final emptiness: death, oblivion. But in this oblivion – the place of the greatest fear – is also the place of the greatest opportunity. The myths teach us that is the God who surrenders to the Goddess. The symbology reveals that it is always the God who dies in the hands of the Goddess of Life. It is he who goes into the Underworld and makes an offering of himself on the altar of Life so the cycle is complete. This imagery of the God offers men the potential for the greatest transformation they will ever be asked to make. Through the surrender to the Goddess, the God gives men the opportunity to release the old forms of self-image and birth the new. Through him men may go beyond dualism and patriarchal patterns of masculinity to initiate into the root source of true masculine power. This is the source that fulfils our deepest dreams. From this death and rebirth, from this willingness to let go, we find a new man. It is here, at the point of sacrifice, that we find a sacred world, balance between the sexes, wholeness of self, exuberant, empowered, incisive male energy, and action that is integrated and harmonious with the all.

Freyr – Norse God of Fertility and earthly abundance. Freyr is the provider of peace and prosperity. Weapons were forbidden in his temples, while his flaming sword could fight on its own accord. He is at home among the elves, dwarves, giants and other nature spirits. He has power in the realm of the dead – that is, among those whose dwelling is within the earth.

The fact that Freyr presides over the earth in conjunction with his sister Freya (Frigg), suggests an extremely early pre-patriarchal origin. Their mother is the ancient Earth Goddess Nerthus. Their names in Old Norse mean 'Lord' and 'Lady.'

Freyr is kin to the Dying and Rising God as, firstly, the myth of Freya has her weeping and otherwise acting in the manner of the Near Eastern goddesses of fertility; secondly, the boar figures strongly in his cult; thirdly, he is a phallic god, a lord of love and sexual activity; and finally, the rites associated with the Scandinavian kings suggest that when they entered the earth, they joined with Freyr, whose spirit then entered into the person of the next king. Freyr is thus reborn in every king, whose annual duty was to undertake the sacrifices necessary for the fertility and prosperity of the people. Freyr was said to be slain by the incoming fiery patriarchal gods.

Pwyll – A Welsh Lord who exchanged places with Arawn, King of the Underworld. Antagonist of Gwydion and ally of the Children of Llyr in their struggle against the Children of Don. Husband of Rhiannon, a Horse Goddess, who are the parents of Pryderi. Pryderi became King of Annwn and Lord of Death after his father. Pwyll introduced the red and white pigs of the Otherworld to this one.

24

The Wheel of the Year

If the Goddess is the field of all things, the swirling vastness visible in the panoply of nature and of space . . . If she is without beginning and without end, the flux of endless universes, then the God is the pathway through it all. He has beginnings, discernible stages along the way, and shows the promise of completion and an end. He is the journey, the marker of the points in the cycle of birth, life and death.

The many faces of the God turn with the cycle of the moon and the cycle of the sun. In the solar cycle, the seed of darkness begins with the turning of the sun at the Summer Solstice. The long journey into the waning half of the year begins. As this is still the part of the year in which the light prevails, there is little development until the Autumnal Equinox. This is the turning point of the year when the God is two-faced. He looks both ways. Neither face is greater than the other, but because the darkness is looming it takes precedence very quickly. At Samhain between October 31 and November 2 – the mid-point or cross-quarter day between Autumn Equinox and Winter Solstice – the darkness comes into its own.

Samhain is the time when the gateway to the Underworld is open. It is possible to walk the labyrinth to the Realm of the Dead, and for the dead to come to us. The Rites of the God include laying out the corpse of the old year – in the Celtic tradition this is the end of the year – and the putting on of the horns of the new. The Stag King inaugurates his rut. Osiris, Adonis, Lugh, are laid in their grave of autumn leaves and the Lord of the Underworld begins his wild dance.

The darkness increases in power until the Winter Solstice. It is then at its peak. This is the time of the shortest day and the longest night – for those of us in the Northern Hemisphere. The Winter Solstice was the calendrical point most awaited for and most marked by our ancestors. It is the time of the root connection with our ancestors in the depth of the cave of earth. Winter Solstice, the winter sun-standstill, connects us with the chthonic power that lies at the root of the Tree of Life. It is the most inner time. The time of the chthonic Red Dragon.

The mystery of life is so organised however, that every extreme contains its own opposite, every zenith its descent, every nadir its ascent. In the same way as the Summer Solstice contains the beginning of the dark, so the Winter Solstice contains the beginning of the light. The sun begins its slow journey back along the horizon and the days become longer. The conception of the light – in darkness – is celebrated. At the mid-point between Winter Solstice and the Vernal Equinox comes the cross-quarter day on or about February 2. This is Imbolc to the Celts, Candlemas in the Christian tradition. The festival has become one that celebrates the return of the light, but in antiquity the focus was on the quickening of the seed in the nurturing darkness of the earth.

The quickening in the dark continues until the Vernal Equinox. Then the dark and light again stand as equals. The God is again two-faced. At Beltane, the next cross-quarter day on or around May 1, the dark is over and all goes rushing to meet the light. The Stag King loses his horns in one last coitus with the Queen of May. He dies so the year can be reborn. The Lord of the Waxing Year increases in power to the peak of mid-summer, the Summer Solstice. Then, in the sky-oriented rites of the light, darkness is again conceived.

None of this rich symbolic cycle is possible without the Goddess. She is there at every step of the way with all her character and complementary rituals. The God and the Goddess go down into the darkness together at Samhain. They meet in the cave of earth at the Winter Solstice to conceive the light. In the same way, the God and the Goddess as Lord and Lady of the waxing vegetation, meet in their fullness at the Summer Solstice, to conceive the dark. Perhaps only at the Equinoxes, the 'equal nights,' does all stand equal and in balance.

This annual pattern suggests various rituals for the God to be carried out at appropriate times. Of course the ritual, say for Winter Solstice, doesn't have to be practiced only then. It may be appropriate at other times. I find that since I began observing the rituals around the turning points of the year, my own cycles of activity correspond closely to them. I conceive and gestate ideas in Winter. They emerge in Spring, culminate over Summer and are released in the Fall. Then I find myself going back down into the depths – often struggling – until my ideas and actions clarify again after the Winter Solstice. I find my relationships and business affairs follow these patterns also. I find the establishment of a sympathetic resonance with the natural cycles of the year to be facilitative, enabling and harmonising, even when it means harmonising with letting go.

The annual cycle or Wheel of the Year provides a backdrop for the rich variety of symbolism necessary for recreating the whole image of the God. It creates a framework that restores the spirit of the divine masculine to the cycle of regeneration. It places the God in the Universe, puts him back into life, alongside the divine feminine power, and places a high value on them all.

The lunar cycle also offers a framework for this. All the stages described above are present in the twenty-nine night lunar cycle: waxing moon, full moon, waning moon and dark moon. The differences between it and the solar cycle are that the lunar cycle is accomplished approximately thirteen times for a single one of the sun, the waxing and waning phases of the moon are explicit, and so is the time of darkness.

The rites of the God in the Universe – not God above and beyond, nor God omnipotent, eternal and omniscient – must include symbolic acts that restore the whole nature to the image of the divine masculine. The God in the Universe is both good and evil, dark and light, wild and ordered, purifying and maddening. The self shares in the same nature. The rites of restoration must constellate within the sense of the masculine a symbolic round in which the God appears as all things. The God journeys around the whole cycle of life. He undergoes the joy and the pain of being born, living and dying. The God gives a name to the unnamable, speech to the unspeakable. He is the voice of death and fear, as well as life and joy. He gives a voice to this in all of life – including the animals, the plants and the otherwise voiceless realms of stars and stones. By the means of his participation in the regenerative cycle of existence he knows all these things, and, by knowing them, he comes to know himself.

The same is true of the Goddess – who is the Universe. The rites of restoration constellate the sense of the feminine as the whole in which the Goddess appears as all things. She is the whole cycle through which the God journeys. The Goddess gives birth, life and death. She is the creation. Through the discovery of herself by the journey of the God, she comes to know herself. The son reveals her depths, her heights. He releases her potential in water, earth, wood and stone. He climbs her mountains, explores her abyss, loves her and is loved by her – loses her and becomes one with her again and again. As well as encompassing good and evil, darkness and light, the rites of restoration must include the balance of masculine and feminine, Lord and Lady, God and Goddess.

The challenge we face at this time however is that there is great imbalance between male and female. This issue must be addressed. For men to meet women as equals, men have to become aware of the privileges they enjoy as a result of current social, political and religious behaviour. Men must voluntarily commit to letting go of patriarchal forms of domination, control, and power-over. Even acknowledging this is an intensely uncomfortable process. It provokes resistance, argument, defensiveness and self-justification. The paradox is that when men finally do let go, they will find all they ever really wanted is there for them: love, support, empowerment, nurturing, belonging, relaxation, trust, sex, and connection with feelings. The restoration of the full image of the divine feminine – the inclusion of her powerful, sexual, earth aspects – and the reconciling of the divided image of the God, provides the exemplary model through mythic imagery for this transformation to happen. A ritual way of dramatising this restoration is described in the next section.

Each of the eight main points in the calendar cycle of the year – the solstices, equinoxes and cross-quarter days – lend themselves to dramatic ritualisation involving the God and Goddess. While the Goddess presents an essential unity through her many aspects, the God may appear as two-fold. He dies and is reborn as God of the Waxing Year and he dies and is reborn as God of the Waning Year. This is also true of the lunar cycle. The God, like the moon, can paradoxically appear as two due to his dying and rising nature. This does not mean the God can be divided into the simple but dangerous dualism of the Near Eastern religions. He must remain in flux, a paradox.

The God of the Waxing Year is conceived at Winter Solstice, quickens (is born?) at Imbolc, is equal to the God of the Waning Year at Spring Equinox, comes into his power at Beltane, is at his peak at Summer Solstice, celebrates his gifts at Lughnasad, is equal to the God of the Waning Year at Autumn Equinox and dies at Samhain. The God of the Waning Year is conceived at Summer Solstice, born at Lughnasad, emerges in his power at Samhain, is at his peak at Winter Solstice, celebrates his gifts at Imbolc and dies at Beltane. There are thus two points in the year for release or surrender – Samhain and Beltane, the beginning of winter and the beginning of summer.

There are variations on this theme or even quite different ways of looking at it. This is the solar form I like to use. Another form that retains the essential unity of the God in his three-stage cycle of rise, maturity and fall, sees the whole year as the wheel. The God is born in the spring and comes to his adulthood in summer. In the autumn he bears his mature gifts, in winter his wisdom. He then dies, to be reborn in the spring. Another form has the God dying and being reborn at the solstices. The cycle is the important factor in whichever variation you prefer.

The festival of Samhain easily lends itself to the challenge of naming and looking at death and projected darkness. The people of countries such as Mexico who have maintained the Day of the Dead ceremonies (November 2) have a head start in meeting the challenge. The nightlong vigil in the cemetery of the ancestors is a pre-conquest indigenous tradition that greatly enhances the now predominantly Christian practice. Yet, because of the prejudice against darkness, the ceremonies are reduced to an inoculation of light against the coming time of dark. They are not an acceptance of darkness itself. In fact most Christian festivals reveal a deep unwillingness to face the 'Cloud of Unknowing' on its own terms. Transcendental monotheism projects its shadow onto others and into teleology – concepts of the 'last days.' The shadow, the dark, death, evil and so on, are externalised in future temporal apocalyptic and millenarian scenarios where unbelievers are doomed and the faithful saved. In the terms of a cosmological linear chronology, there can be no original absolute creator without a final absolute destruction. There was a beginning, therefore there must be an end. Many of the holders of these concepts are, unfortunately, hastening to prove the truth of their own beliefs. The concentration camps were a dramatic fulfillment of Nazi apocalyptic ideology. One may justly fear that the predicted teleological extinctions found within the desert religions – Christianity, Judaism and Islam – may be fulfilled if their fundamentalist extremes predominate.

In contrast, the native pagan traditions always included a close relationship with the cycle of life and death. These traditions were not filled with distant teleological abstractions based on faith, but on immediate, earth-honouring and life-affirming practices. The widespread mortuary practices of prehistoric Europe for example reveal elaborate funeral ritual. These included the leaving out of the body, then dismemberment, inhumation, and articulation of the bones in a collective ossuary. Rituals for the dead probably went on over the entire year, with greater focus at particular times. The megalithic passage graves – 4,000-2,000 B.C.E. (approx.) – for example, appear to have been cleaned out and new bones put in only every few years, or even only every few decades. The bones lay outside for everyone to see, but their subsequent careful articulation shows this was not a practice of neglect. The facing of the dead brought death into the regenerative cycle whereby the community could regularly achieve a collective atonement, a unity with the ancestors, integration of the shadow, a cathartic release, and a sense of the whole. Such practices suggest a worldview utterly different from the achievement of individual salvation within a linear framework of time.

Wild Herdsman – The Wild Herdsman appears early in the European tradition. Closely related to Cernunnos, the Bachlach and the Gruagach, the Wild Herdsman is the Guardian of Nature and Lord of the Animals. He guards an entrance to the Underworld. This is usually located within a green mound – an ancient tumulus. Frequently there is a tree, a spring or fountain nearby. The Wild Herdsman has a formidable appearance. He is a giant with a mighty club. Often described as black, one-eyed, and one-legged he challenges and tests those who would approach his domain.

Hades – The Greek God of the Underworld and Death. Hades presides over the burial and the judgement of the deceased. To avoid speaking his name and to emphasise his positive characteristics the Greeks called him Plouton or Pluto the 'giver of wealth.' In this aspect Hades is a beneficent chthonian God dispensing wealth and fertility from out of the earth. Hades is generally depicted enthroned with his Queen Persephone surrounded by the fruits of the land. Hades is the son of Cronos and Rhea, and brother of Poseidon and Zeus. The three brothers cast lots to see who should rule the Underworld, the Sky and the Sea. Hades drew the Underworld. The many-headed Hound of Hell, Cerberus, guards the entrance to Hades' domain. He never lets anyone leave lightly. Hades has a serpent form, that among other reasons has contributed to his unpopular image. It is implied that every winter he abducts Persephone, when in fact it is a celebratory reunion.

25

The Return of the Gods

The God teaches us to open the furrow in the black earth so the fertility of the field can come forth. He is the harrow in the hand of the farmer. He is the pruner in the hand of the vine-keeper. He is the axe that destroys life to sustain it – to provide fires, to build lodges and to take it on ships across dark seas. The God teaches us about the vulnerability and the ephemeral nature of power. His rites teach us to reach out beyond the present to build upon the Field of the Goddess, but not to hold on or be attached to any outcome.

This closing section of the book offers some practical ways to bring about the return of the Gods.

Naming the God

The return of the God begins with the courage to name his many aspects. The naming of the aspects of the God begins with the earth. Through the awareness that everything inanimate partakes in the nature of the God it is possible to begin the work of reclaiming the sacredness of the earth. Giving voice to his presence transforms the rocks, the woods, the streets, the iron bridges, the ships, the rivers, the oceans, the winds. They become at one with the mysterious cycle of the whole. The presence of the God as the Destroyer, as the dancing Death-bringer – as the end of the planet and the sun, as the end of the universe itself – promises the radical transformation of everything, even down to the tiniest sub-atomic particle.

This is also true for every animate and sentient thing. Everything will die, without exception. As a part of the God it is possible to begin the work of reclaiming the sacredness of mortal life. Naming his presence in animate life transforms the deer, the mouse, the seal, the birds, the insects, the snake, the whales, the plankton, the trees, the life of the cells. Naming his presence within us transforms us. We are one within the mystery of the whole. The presence of the God as the Destroyer, as the dancing Death-bringer – as the end of the life of every sentient thing, as the end of our life – promises the total transformation of our lives, even down to the tiniest thought or consequence of our actions.

Create a safe space. Prepare it how you please. Call in whatever you need to make it sacred. Sit in a circle if you are with company. Note the time of year, the phase of the moon, the passage of the seasons. Call in the God and Goddess appropriate to the time.

Name the Goddess. Shape her aspects. See how she is dressed and what she carries. Feel her presence. Hear her songs, and sing them back to her. Honour her gifts, her wholeness – the divine feminine power within.

Name the God. Call upon all his names. Feel the qualities of each. Give them a shape, a form. See his attributes and appearance as each presence draws in. Allow him to be all things. Name his dark aspects and his light aspects. Name his goodness and his wickedness. Let him be whole – the divine masculine power within.

Know that both God and Goddess exist within you.

Coming to our Senses

Restoring the God is not so much a question of coming to new ideas and definitions about him as it is coming to our senses. The God lives in our bodies. He is alive in the ancient memory of our cells. He is present in the feelings and actions that have been and frequently still are denied their relationship with the divine.

With your non-dominant hand, for most of us the left or 'sinister' hand, draw a picture of the God. It can be abstract, symbolic or whatever you feel represents his image. This approach departs from the mind and enters the realm of the unconscious and non-rational memory.

Again with your non-dominant hand, draw a picture of the youthful, rising God. The mature, powerful God. The old, wise descending God. The Light God. The Dark God. The Trickster. The Guide. Arrange the pictures in any order that is meaningful to you.

Other approaches may include dressing in the costume, skins, mask or horns of whichever aspect of the God you wish to work with. Through bodily movement, by going out into the wilds, through feeling the power of nature and of place, by dramatising or re-enacting an episode from the myth cycle of a God, we experience the radical and ecstatic. The images, movements, and sounds of the deep unconscious, are released from the cellular memory.

What would it mean to you to fashion a mask of the Green Man, drape yourself with his leaves, and dance at the return of spring? What would it mean to bear the horns of Cernunnos or of Pan at a festival of thanksgiving for summer abundance? What would it mean to get up and speak for the rights of animals or for the development of sustainable technology at an academic conference in autumn? What would it mean to don the green hat of Robin Hood in winter and protect the Wild Wood from those who would harm it? It is more than simply being a spectator at the few places in Europe that still remember these things. It is rebirth – a re-connection with the power of life in the cycles of Nature. It is reforging – a re-making of a true spiritual tradition. It is magic – the use of will in concert with ancestral memory and the power of place to effect transformation.

The Altar of the God

If you wish to take physical activity further, build an altar to the God. Allow yourself plenty of time to visualise the altar. Allow it to take form in your mind. The images of the God may express your wildness, your sexuality, your pain, your grief, your anger, your joy, your humour, or your love. You may choose the develop the aspect of the God you feel is missing in your life. It may be difficult to access the trickster for example as he is divorced from our image of the sacred in the West, but by focusing on this aspect of the God and expressing it in the practice of altar building the qualities of the trickster will become present.

If you feel the missing qualities lie in the realm of the shadow it may be hard to go beyond the images of fear. Meditate deeply on these images. Find out exactly what they are trying to say to you. Remember the test of the initiate is always one of facing fear. Examine the images as they arise. Breathe into them. Hold the inviolable centre of your heart. Go through the fear. And if you look back, you will see it was only an image painted on a screen.

The God has many forms. He will take you into the Underworld. He will take you into the animal world. He will take you to death and rebirth. He is a shape-shifter. He is slippery. He may suggest abominable things. Think on them. Make them conscious. Facing the whole nature of the God means releasing dreams, accessing suppressed feelings, discovering new sources of energy, creativity and fertility.

When ready, create the altar. Find objects that express what you found in meditation. The altar does not have to be large. It does need to be in a quiet and undisturbed space so its qualities build up over a period of time. You will find that what you give to the altar will be there when you need it. The more care and attention you give it, the more care and attention there will be for you. Eventually you may not need to keep the altar. It has done its work.

Journey to the Underworld

If the aspect of the God you would like to develop in your life is about the shadow, you may make a journey into the Underworld using a visualisation from an established spiritual tradition. Select the tradition that feels closest to you. Allow yourself to be guided by Hermes, by Gwynn ap Nudd, by the deities of the Egyptian or the American traditions. The Celtic Avalonian imagery suggests an otherworldly island, ships and riders, hounds and cauldrons, apples and sleeping monarchs. The Egyptian tradition suggests animal-headed guides, a river, great temples, a Hall of Judgment, the weighing of the soul, tests and esoteric wisdom. Native American traditions suggest the animal powers, the elemental spirits of the directions, the world of nature and the ancestors. Allow the rich symbols of the tradition to soak into your consciousness and see where they take you. Follow the one that feels closest to you, or follow them all, or none of them.

Maybe it is possible to converse with an ancestor, an enthroned deity, a power... to find a source of untapped potential and creativity... to find words, images, relationship, scents, colours, objects... to go into a cave and paint images from your somatic memory of the life powers... to put them on, take them in, and return with them to this world.

A struggle may be necessary. There is a guardian of our fears. It assumes the form of the forces you find hostile in the world: a violent storm, a poisonous serpent, an impassable waste, a vicious dog... allowing, accepting, moving through them may reveal the shape of evil itself. What form does it take for you? How does it manifest in your world? What is the most positive way in which this evil can be faced and integrated?

Perhaps a death is needed. A dying to the old self, or aspects of the self. A dismemberment, a hanging upon a tree, a decapitation, a sloughing of old skin. Perhaps it is enough merely not to know. To allow the images to subside – to slide into darkness, to sleep, to dream. What happens? What is there? What or who returns?

Reconciling the God

If you like to work with visualisation I offer the following journey to assist in filling out all the aspects of the God and reconciling his divided imagery.

Create a sacred space. Relax your body and close your eyes. See a pathway descending before you. Follow it down until you come to a portal, an opening. Pass through it. You are in the Underworld domain of the Goddess and the God. On this journey go toward the God. See him surrounded by his attributes and the things meaningful to you. What does he look like?

If it is helpful, recall some of characteristics of the God described in this book: The Horned God. God of Fertility. Protector of Nature. Guardian of Animals. Guide to the Underworld. Rider of the Wild Hunt. Lord of the Necropolis. Shape shifter. Trickster. The God of Games.

When you have a clear image of the God, return by the way you came. Through the opening. Up the pathway. Return to your sacred space. Now comes the next stage.

See a pathway ascending before you. Follow it up until you come to a portal, an opening. Pass through. You are in the Heavenly realm of the Solar Goddess and the Light God. On this journey go toward the Light God. See him surrounded by his attributes and the things he means to you. What does he look like?

If it helps, recall some of the characteristics commonly attributed to the Light God: Sky God. Thunder and Lightning God. God of Creativity. Harvest God. God of energy, fire and of warriors. Whatever imagery is personal to you.

When you have a clear image of the Light God, return by the way you came. Through the opening. Down the pathway. Return to your sacred space.

Now hold both the Light God and the God in your visualisation. See them both in their respective places. Then visualise the phases of the moon. See the waxing moon, the full moon, the waning moon, and the dark moon. Take the time you need to do that, and hold the image of the lunar phases before you.

Invite the God to take his place in the lunar cycle.

Invite the Light God to take his place in the lunar cycle.

See them both take their places in the cycle of the whole.

As the phases of the moon turn around their cycle, see the aspects of the God turning. See the divided aspects of the God coming into wholeness and conciliation at full moon and dark moon.

When you are ready, leave this unified image of the God. Whenever you wish to see it again, all you have to do is return to this sacred space.

Close the sacred space. Return to present time.

Surrender to the Goddess

At least once in the story of each God named in this book there is a surrender to the Goddess. The lovely Adonis springs up, is adored by women, and fades away. Shiva dies in sexual embrace with Kali. Cernunnos sheds his horns. Dionysos is torn apart by the Maenads. The breast of Robin Hood is pierced by arrows in the greenwood bower he shares with Mari-Anna. Baal meets his end on the threshing floor of the Great Goddess, Anat, Astarte or Asherah. They all go into the Underworld. The examples are numerous and suggest ways in which men can let go of the ingrained, hard-wired male patterns of goal-achievement, domination and control.

The purpose of the following ritual is for men to align themselves to the aspect of the sacred masculine able to let go. This is the aspect of the psyche that goes into the Underworld — that aligns itself with the transformational character of the God. Patterns or self-definitions that no longer serve are released. The male need to do, to achieve, to be something or someone in order to exist, is jettisoned. The deepest fears surrounding the self are allowed, acknowledged and surrendered to. The possibility is that the man will be reborn. As the Goddess, the Great Mother, gives birth to all, this rebirth can happen only through surrender to her. The image of the divine masculine can die and be reborn into wholeness only through the whole image of the divine feminine. The result is that the man will find a new male sense of self from which he can act in harmony with the feminine and with all life.

Work this ritual at an appropriate time of year: Beltane, Samhain, the Winter Solstice, the Dark of the Moon. Work it in appropriate surroundings: the wilderness, the woods, a safe sacred space. If possible work it with friends or a ritual group willing to enact the various figures. But the form I first describe is done alone. Make the ritual work for you. Use whatever you need to make it real. Follow whatever clues are given, especially by the senses and the feelings of your body.

First, create a sacred space dedicated to the feminine. Decorate the space with objects to represent the significant women in your life. Use pictures of your mother, friends, lovers, children. Bring in something to represent any women you have interacted with in your life and around whom there is something incomplete, some energy. If you wish to, create an altar to the Goddess. Do whatever is necessary to create an entranceway, a transition zone to this place.

145

Second, create a sacred space dedicated to the masculine. Create an altar to the God. Adorn it with male power objects. Bring something to represent your father or other significant men in your life. Bring in things that represent significant achievements, or failures, on your part as a man. Wear costume, a mask or nothing at all. Use body paint, mud, charcoal. Then wait.

When you feel invited, move from the male to the female sacred space. Feel the transition in your body. Don't push your way in. You must feel your way in. What is it like to enter the women's area? Go around the circle acknowledging the presence of the women. Remember your history with them. Put yourself into their place as a woman. See from their eyes. Take time to do this. Then, as yourself, tell them something you are ashamed of that you did to a woman. Tell them the most painful thing you ever did to a woman or women. Bear the consequences. Listen to the response. Surrender to it.

When the women's space is done with you, move back to the male sacred area. What do you now feel about the altar to the God? Do you want to make any changes to it? How do you feel about the other objects there? Re-arrange them to accord with your experience. Enact the change with your body. What do you personally intend to do to end your patriarchal privileges?

Finally, if you are fortunate to have a circle of men and women who will support you in this ritual talk with them about enacting it together. This will make it much more powerful. It will become a shared expiation of patriarchy. The women will create the female sacred space. You and your men friends will create the male. Talk with the men about what the objects you bring mean to you. When the women invite you, enter their circle. Get down to the task immediately. Feel it. This is not a confession or a mental exercise. Get real. Tell the women exactly what you have done to a woman that is most painful to you. Listen to and feel their response.

Surrender to this ritual. Don't intellectualise it. Don't say to yourself, "that part's O.K. But I disagree with that part." Hear what the women say or do by responding with your feelings and your body. The women need to be careful to respond to the man's surrender and not solely to their projections as a result of their experience of men. When the women are done with you and let you go back to the men's circle, interact with the men to express your experience. Adapt the ritual to work for you. As the point of this ritual is surrender to the feminine don't try and control the ritual in any way. If the women chose to do something entirely different, let go to it.

Alternatively, work the ritual with just men. Create the sacred spaces together. Then, when working the space dedicated to the feminine, each man's process will be witnessed in turn by the circle of men.

This ritual is not a disempowerment of men. It is a disempowerment of patriarchal forms of masculinity. Only then, when these old forms are released, will men and women come to be human beings in harmony within the whole. The return of the symbolism of the God offers one of the most powerful means I know of for accomplishing this much needed transformation on the planet today.

The Demands of the Gods

After I did the ritual described above, I had a vivid image of an angry set of Gods entering my mind. It was as though they had formed a union to protest the monopoly of one of their number! They were especially upset about the damage to life and the environment while they had been away. They presented me with a set of four demands that they felt could begin the process of restoration. I record these as follows:

1. The relinquishing of all 'holy' books and dogmas about religion and the God.
2. The end of all meaningless and sterile debates over the rightness and wrongness of theology, doctrine and belief, and the upholding and validation of every individual's spiritual experience.
3. The release of the hold by a single religion on the spiritual places of the people. The opening up of all sacred places for spiritual use by the people.
4. The taking of vows by those who wish to serve the spiritual needs of the people that include the upholding of the above points, and

which honour each individual and serve his or her needs in whatever form they may be.

I think by the last point the Gods meant it was OK for someone to study a traditional spiritual system or practice and offer it to any who thought they would benefit from it, but not to uphold it as the only system, the only way. The idea was that those who wished to serve people's spiritual needs must be open to all traditions, regardless of their own personal beliefs.

I think by number 3 the Gods were suggesting something quite radical. I think it was recognising that people have spiritual needs, especially at times of birth, crisis, transition and death, and that the places now dedicated to serving those needs should relinquish their hold on a single faith and open their doors to everyone. I believe the Unitarian Church already practice something like this. Their buildings are open to serve their congregations regardless of spiritual belief. The symbols of all faiths are present in their churches and the services reflect this plurality. I think in these demands, the Gods were asking for a democracy of religion rather than a tyranny or a monopoly, for something that served the people rather than imposing itself upon them. If your imagination was to see the returning Gods, what do you think they would say? Would it be drastically different to the points above, or would they wish to add more?

The Return of the God

We close the book by remembering that the most ancient image of the sacred manifested in the world by human consciousness takes the form of the Goddess. She emerges in different forms in every age, mirroring the self back to the self. From the Palaeolithic to the Bronze Age she appears with all her aspects. She is Earth Mother, Mistress of the Animals, Queen of Heaven, Life-Giver and Life-Taker. She is the embodiment of nature and of the human soul. She performs the Sacred Marriage with the God.

From the Iron Age to the recent present the Goddess was merely Virgin Mother. But now, the rapid restoration of all her aspects by human consciousness – especially that of Earth Mother – means that she, and we, are now in a position to birth a new image of her son. We are ready to restore all the aspects of the God. In the past the God has appeared as a redeeming saviour, as the sacred king sacrificing himself for his people, as the solar hero defeating darkness, and as the dying and rising spirit of fertility and vegetation, but as we do the work to restore all the aspects of the divine masculine, in what form will the God appear this time?

Visualise the divine feminine, the Great Goddess. See her in all her forms: In Ice Age figurines, Neolithic sculpture, the Egyptian Isis, the Greek Demeter, Hecate, Aphrodite, the Indian Parvati, Kali, the Christian Mary, Sophia, Magdalene, the American White Buffalo Woman, Corn Mother, the Celtic Rhiannon, Cerridwen. She is Queen of Earth, Heaven and the Underworld. She is maiden, mother, crone. She is beautiful, sexual and terrifying. Her gown is made up of stars, of shells, of trees, of bones, of flowing waters. Birds play in her hair, wolves and lions at her hands and serpents at her feet. She gives birth to all things and to her all things return.

She is preparing to give birth. She opens up her body. She shakes and trembles as she begins the birth pangs. She is in ecstasy. The winds roar around her. The oceans rush forward. The trees bow down before her efforts. The creatures draw back in awe.

At the threshold of her womb a male figure appears. Who is he? What does he look like? What aspects does he have? What does he bring that you have been longing for?

Pay attention to him. What does he look like? Does he manifest aspects that identify him with any of the themes described in this book? If so, it may be helpful to study this theme, or themes, for help in understanding why he is appearing to you in this way now.

The God may appear in several forms – as Earth God, as Guardian, as Animal God, as a Wrathful God, as Wisdom Keeper and so on – or in one universal form. Pay attention to all his manifestations. They will tell you about yourself. He may appear to bring attention to a side of yourself you are neglecting. He may appear to tell you about the archetypal aspects of life you are most concerned with now. He may be something entirely new and uncertain. What makes the experience certain is when the imagery is compelling, whole-making, complete, possessing such archetypal qualities as polarity, symmetry and four-foldness

The God may appear with a partner, his lover. This may help illuminate his character, or it may tell you something about your life now. However he appears, once you have encountered his compelling archetypal form, this is the aspect of the God you are working with in your life now. The God may change over time, or present different faces to you. He may appear in dreams, in synchronicities, or in meditations. Be assured that the more you bring him into your consciousness the greater the understanding of your life. Through the restoration of all the faces of the divine masculine, the richer your life will be.

Bibliography

Adam Douglas, *The Beast Within*, London, Chapmans Publishers, 1992.

Alan Bleakley, *Fruits of the Moon Tree*, London, Gateway Books, 1984.

Alice K. Turner, *The History of Hell,* Harcourt Brace & Co., 1993.

Anne Baring & Jules Cashford, *The Myth of the Goddess*, Viking, 1991.

Anne Ross, *Pagan Celtic Britain*, London, Routledge & Kegan Paul, 1967.

Barbara G. Walker, *The Women's Encyclopedia of Myths and Secrets,* Harper San Francisco, 1983.

Dudley Young, *Origins of the Sacred: The Ecstasies of Love and War*, New York, HarperCollins, 1991.

Hilda Ellis Davidson, *Myths and Symbols in Pagan Europe: Early Scandinavian and Celtic Religions,* Syracuse University Press, 1988.

Jeffrey Burton Russell, (1) *The Devil: Perceptions of Evil from Antiquity to Primitive Christianity*, Ithaca, Cornell University Press, 1977.

(2) *The Prince of Darkness: Radical Evil and the Power of Good in History*, Ithaca, Cornell University Press, 1988.

John Gray, *Near Eastern Mythology*, New York, Peter Bedrick Books, 1982.

John Matthews, Ed., *Choirs of the God: Revisioning Masculinity*, London, Mandala, 1991.

John Rowan, *The Horned God: Feminism and Men as Wounding and Healing,* London, Routledge, 1987.

Marija Gimbutas, (1) *The Language of the Goddess*, San Francisco, Harper & Row, 1989.

(2) *The Civilization of the Goddess: The World of Old Europe*, San Francisco, HarperCollins, 1991.

Mary Midgley, *Wickedness: A Philosophical Essay*, London, Routledge & Kegan Paul, 1984.

Mircea Eliade. All of Eliade's works, and those which he is editor, provide invaluable resource material on the themes of the God.

Morris Berman, *Coming to Our Senses*, New York, Bantam, 1990.

Nicholas R. Mann, (1) *His Story: Masculinity in the Post-Patriarchal World*, St. Paul, Llewellyn, 1995.

(2) *The Dark God*, St. Paul, Llewellyn1996.

(3) *The Isle of Avalon*, Green Magic, 2001.

(4) .... & Marcia Sutton, *Giants of Gaia*, Albuquerque, Brotherhood of Life, 1995.

R. J. Stewart, (1) *Celtic Gods and Goddesses*, London, Blandford Press, 1990.

(2) *The Bright One Unmasked: Celebrating the Male Mysteries*, Bath, Arcana, 1991.

Ralph Metzner, *The Well of Remembrance*, Boston, Shambhala, 1994.

Robert Lawlor, *Earth Honoring: The New Male Sexuality*, Rochester, Park Street Press, 1989.

Sogyal Rinpoche, *The Tibetan Book of Living and Dying*, San Francisco, HarperCollins, 1992.

Starhawk, *Dreaming the Dark*, Boston, Beacon Press, 1982.

Index

Numbers in bold type indicate a section with a description of the god

153